W9-CPA-183

GETTING WHAT YOU WANT

HOW TO REACH AGREEMENT
AND RESOLVE CONFLICT EVERY TIME

KARE ANDERSON

A PLUME BOOK

PLUME
Published by the Penguin Group
Penguin Books USA Inc., 375 Hudson Street, New York, New York 10014, U.S.A.
Penguin Books Ltd, 27 Wrights Lane, London W8 5TZ, England
Penguin Books Australia Ltd, Ringwood, Victoria, Australia
Penguin Books Canada Ltd, 10 Alcorn Avenue,
Toronto, Ontario, Canada M4V 3B2
Penguin Books (N.Z.) Ltd, 182–190 Wairau Road, Auckland 10, New Zealand

Penguin Books Ltd, Registered Offices: Harmondsworth, Middlesex, England

Published by Plume, an imprint of Dutton Signet,
a division of Penguin Books USA Inc. Previously published in a Dutton edition.

First Plume Printing, February, 1994
10 9 8 7 6 5 4 3 2 1

Copyright © Kare Anderson, 1993
All rights reserved

 REGISTERED TRADEMARK—MARCA REGISTRADA

LIBRARY OF CONGRESS CATALOGING-IN-PUBLICATION DATA
Anderson, Kare.
    Getting what you want : how to reach agreement and resolve
conflicts every time / Kare Anderson.
        p.   cm.
    ISBN 0-452-27053-7
    1. Negotiation.   2. Interpersonal conflict.   3. Conflict
management.   I. Title.
    BF637.N4A5   1994
    158'.5—dc20   93–23437
                                                        CIP

Printed in the United States of America
Original hardcover design by Leonard Telesca

Without limiting the rights under copyright reserved above, no part of this
publication may be reproduced, stored in or introduced into a retrieval system, or
transmitted, in any form, or by any means (electronic, mechanical, photocopying,
recording, or otherwise), without the prior written permission of both the
copyright owner and the above publisher of this book.

BOOKS ARE AVAILABLE AT QUANTITY DISCOUNTS WHEN USED TO PROMOTE PRODUCTS
OR SERVICES. FOR INFORMATION PLEASE WRITE TO PREMIUM MARKETING DIVISION,
PENGUIN BOOKS USA INC., 375 HUDSON STREET, NEW YORK, NEW YORK 10014

HOW TO MOVE TOWARD PEACE, NOT WAR, TO GET WHAT YOU WANT

In *Getting What You Want*, highly successful communications expert Kare Anderson teaches Triangle Talk, a revolutionary three-step method to reach better agreements more easily in everyday life. Anderson has perfected 100 direct techniques to make the "getting what you want" process an ingrained habit, a reflex that overcomes prejudices, suspicions, and anger between two parties. Triangle Talk works—in the office and the home—to ensure that negotiation is always a win-win situation.

GETTING WHAT YOU WANT

"Gloriously easy to read . . . enlightens the reader on every page." —Jay Conrad Levinson, author of *Guerilla Marketing Weapons*

"*Getting What You Want*'s three steps make great sense for everyone. [Kare Anderson] has isolated the items at the core of interpersonal communication." —Jim Cathcart, author of *Relationship Selling*

"This book is for everyone who's ever felt that rise of anger or intimidation where they knew they were going to do the wrong thing." —Roger Dawson, author of *The Confident Decisionmaker*

KARE ANDERSON is president of Anderson Negotiations/Communications, Inc., and a full-time speaker on leadership skills like influence, conflict resolution, and constituency building. She has worked with such diverse groups as Syntex, Nomuro Securities, Ringling Brothers & Barnum & Bailey Circus, and the American Library Association. She lives in Tiburon, California.

You cannot defect from an insight.
You cannot unsee what you have seen.
—MARTIN LUTHER KING, JR.

This book is dedicated to *seeing* a new picture
of what we can do differently when we get
frustrated with that other person:

When love is gone we turn to justice.
When justice is gone we turn to power.
When power is gone we turn to violence.

To Lestelle and Arnold

Your most important lessons were taught
without words:

Have convictions. Make your choices based
on them.

Recognize how every choice shapes you and *every*
interaction leaves its mark on you.

It is equally important to be good while doing the
right thing as it is to actually do the right thing.

Look to someone's highest side, especially when
disagreeing with them.

Remain constant in your loving.

Problems seldom exist
at the level at which they are presented.
—Zen saying

The opposite of a fact is a falsehood,
but the opposite of one profound truth
may very well be another profound truth.
—NIELS BOHR

ACKNOWLEDGMENTS

When trying to reach agreements, we always find a shorter path when we seek the truth beneath the apparent truth. Several people have helped teach me that, often not in any way they intended. However, we seldom get the gifts we want in the packages we can most easily recognize, or even at the right times. Only looking back does the pattern emerge. Looking back now, here are some of the bright tracers who helped illuminate my way.

These are some of the inspiring researchers and writers whose work helped clear a path for me: Robert Trout, for reaching agreements that don't slash and burn; Robert Cialdini, for research on why people instinctively say yes; Harriet Goldhor Lerner, for her insight on anger; Alfie Kohn, for his groundbreaking argument against competition; Robert Bramson, the best and first to talk about responding to difficult people; Morris Berman, for his large-picture view of how our mind/body split is leading us adrift; Deborah Tannen, for explaining why women and men are having difficulty hearing each other; and Stephen Covey, for his advocacy of a return to character first, technique second.

My agent, Patti Breitman, whose passionate championship of everything in which she believes was a model of behavior, as was her integrity and constant ability to focus. It is a luxury to have her as my critic and advocate.

Connie Lee Merritt, for helping me practice telling the immediate truth in business and in friendship.

My very sweet baby sister Melinda, for shining her beacon light down from Oregon.

Judith Brown, for her clarity, subtlety, and her willingness to be vulnerable and for her invariable search for the less obvious.

Thelton Eugene Henderson, witness for justice and my "rock of ages."

George McLaird, whose sermons taught me to shine a light on my shadow side to see the undeveloped "other characters" residing within, so that I could become acquainted with them and thus be less surprised when they presented themselves through other people.

Carol Costello, who has more people residing inside her than most any other sane person I know and who makes each voice come out separately and pared down on the written page.

Lily Hills, for her ability to keep on giving.

Paul Ekman, whose extraordinary research and writing on faces, lying, and grief opened my eyes to new ways to reach agreement.

Paul Geffner, who speaks words like "they taste good" and always returns to play.

Robert Sciutto, the "scout" who seeks out the right action by instinct.

Natalie Wooler, forced-to-be-wise-old-soul-at-age-eight who will dance and play flirt to bring out even the most cynical person's sweetest side.

Mac Carter, for spirit.

CONTENTS

FOREWORD

I have watched Kare Anderson teach her method for reaching agreements to a wide variety of people, including medical school deans, sales executives, and professional athletes. I teach negotiation skills for a living, and even I gained invaluable insights and effective techniques from this approach. It works for everyone.

Kare's method, which she calls Triangle Talk, is based on the premise that no negotiation will work if it is based on manipulation or chicanery. Triangle Talk works because every party in a Triangle Talk negotiation comes away feeling that they were heard, that they were understood, and that their needs are going to be met.

Kare's style is personal and down-to-earth, reflecting a healthy and honest approach to negotiating. In no other book on the subject will you find advice that works so well in every aspect of life.

Triangle Talk shows us how to maintain our boundaries and meet our needs while making sure our "adversaries" are getting their own "bottom line" needs met. Everyone feels good after a Triangle Talk negotiation. And anyone who practices this technique in his personal and professional life will feel significantly more in control than people who just muddle through from one frustrating negotiation to the next.

So many of us project our own fears and motivations on others. In *Getting What You Want*, you will learn how to recognize your own blind spots and why you have the most trouble reaching agreement with the people for whom you have the strongest feelings.

You are about to learn the most simple and effective skills for managing your own feelings and getting what you want in any negotiation. Congratulations on taking this important step toward conflict resolution with integrity, grace, and success!

Roger Dawson
author of *You Can Get Anything You Want, Secrets of Power Negotiating, Secrets of Power Persuasion*

HOW TO GET WHAT YOU WANT:
Triangle Talk

WHY TRIANGLE TALK WORKS:
Six Payoffs

Eighty percent of us believe that we are in the top
ten percent of how well we get along with others.
—1989 Gallup poll

* Do you ever avoid saying what you want or how you feel
  for fear of how someone will react?
* Do people stop listening before you stop talking? Do
  people ignore or interrupt you? Do you want people to
  listen more closely and respect what you say more?
* Are you caught in the same unsatisfying "scripts," conversations, or arguments that seem to repeat themselves
  and go around in circles?
* Do you feel either too aggressive or too reticent when
  you approach people about agreements or problems?
* Do certain kinds of people make it almost impossible for
  you to communicate effectively? Do you know the secret
  of relating to and working with people who—

. . . Always turn the conversation back to *their* needs, *their*
experiences, and *their* reactions?
. . . Try to make you feel guilty?
. . . Yell, make hostile remarks, or habitually interrupt or
complain?

. . . Stare at you blankly, with no expression or response, even when you ask them direct questions?

. . . Misrepresent you or your views to others?

. . . Want everybody (but especially you) to like them, and so agree with everything?

This book offers a simple, elegant solution, what I call Triangle Talk. This method will give you powerful skills in conflict resolution, negotiation, and persuasion so that you can get more of what you want in both your professional and your personal life. You will learn how to cut through tension, frustration, or confusion in any situation, and to resolve disagreements so that everyone feels satisfied.

Triangle Talk lets you express your own wants and needs in ways that intrigue people, rather than alienate them. It gives you a lifelong, universal tool for turning conflict into cooperation, producing solid agreements that work for everyone, and building relationships grounded in mutual consideration and respect.

Powerful Steps

Triangle Talk is based on first knowing your own specific needs and wants in any given situation, so that you can next listen better to other people's needs and wants, let them know that you have heard them, and then find a genuine common ground.

The three Triangle Talk steps are:

1. Know *exactly* what you want.
2. Find out what they want and make them feel heard.
3. Propose action in a way they can accept.

These steps form a triangle, the visual image you can use to trigger the Triangle Talk habit and make it a way of life.

Whenever you start to negotiate or feel a conflict surfacing, use the proven power of visual imagery and remember this triangle. Let the triangle guide you through the three steps

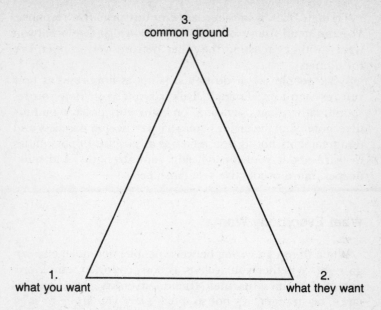

3.
common ground

1.
what you want

2.
what they want

and move you from confusion to clarity, from negative feelings to solid connections with others.

Make the triangle your anchor no matter what the circumstances—an important salary negotiation, a volatile staff meeting, a strategy session with a client, an encounter with a difficult customer, even a situation in which you are taken by surprise or find yourself uncomfortably involved with people about whom you have strong feelings.

Fight, Flight, or Triangle Talk

Most of us react to conflict the same way our ancient ancestors reacted to saber-toothed tigers appearing on the horizon. Our instinct is still "fight or flight," however much we have evolved in other areas. Our primitive urge is either to fight back and escalate the conflict, or to run away. This flight may mean actually leaving the room, or simply withdrawing emotionally. When you give in to either fight or flight, you lose control of the situation and are likely to feel either abusive or victimized.

Triangle Talk is an alternative to this primitive response. You can stand your ground, hold your own, and get what you want—without roasting the other person over an open fire for dinner.

What people say or do to you is not as important as how you respond to it. Triangle Talk lets you *choose* how you respond, rather than operating "on automatic" or letting others determine your behavior. You will start seeing conflicts and disagreements not as disasters, but as positive opportunities to learn about yourself, develop your strengths, and build deeper, more productive relationships.

What Everybody Wants

When things go wrong between people, not much else can go right. Whether your role is as boss, coworker, employee, potential business partner, friend, adversary, new acquaintance, or stranger, it's not so much *where* you argue or *what* you argue about as *how* you argue that determines how you feel about yourself and others, and how they feel about you.

We all want to be heard and respected, to say what we want and feel without jeopardizing our relationships with the people who are important to us. We want to express ourselves freely and fully, get the results we want, and at the same time maintain and nurture our connections with others.

Triangle Talk is designed to do just that.

Six Big Payoffs

Triangle Talk gives you a unique combination of advantages:

1. It can be applied in any situation.

Triangle Talk gives you a universal, baseline response to any challenging situation. You can use it—

- At home or at work.
- Whether you are cool and detached, or emotionally involved.

- With anyone you encounter—your CEO, an employee, a distracted salesperson, even a child, spouse, or parent.
- When you are taken by surprise, or when you have time to prepare.

Life has become too complex, too filled with unexpected flashes of conflict, for methods that require advance planning or rigid emotional control. Only an approach that is instinctive and habitual and can be applied universally on the spur of the moment will work.

2. It is clear and easy to use.

You don't need an M.B.A. to master this approach; you just need to remember the three points of a triangle.

3. It is based on honesty and mutual support, not *on coercion or manipulation.*

Triangle Talk is not about swimming with the sharks and making canned tuna of anyone who crosses you. It is about knowing what you genuinely want and putting yourself and your ideas forward so that you succeed and the people around you succeed as well.

Triangle Talk is designed to strengthen your relationships, to build connections that are authentic, supportive, and effective—not to generate more friction or frustration.

It gives you a perfect balance of assertiveness and receptivity. You get results, not revenge or escalation.

You and the other person are more apt to respect, and perhaps even to like, one another after the agreement is reached. You have found a way to talk and work things out. This bond makes both of you more comfortable and confident, and more likely to engage in the process again—between yourselves and with others.

Few of our institutions—family, church, government, or business—look the way they did ten years ago. There is less agreement on common values and acceptable modes of behavior. Sometimes it's hard to know what the rules are now, let alone follow them. The three Triangle Talk steps ground you in a set of standards that are both ethical and highly effective.

4. It works from the inside out.

Triangle Talk makes life less stressful because it is based

on knowing your own authentic wants and needs. You don't have to figure out what role to play; you simply tell the truth.

5. You get good agreements that stick.

Your agreements are based on what you want, and what others want. They are less likely to backfire because they benefit both of you and you've both participated in making them.

The five hallmarks of a good agreement are:

1. The agreement lasts.
2. All parties think it is the best possible compromise.
3. Your circumstances are no worse than they were before the agreement was reached, and may be better.
4. Coming to an agreement leaves you in a better position than not coming to an agreement.
5. You don't win the battle and lose the war. You won't experience backlash or worse conditions in the future because of this agreement.

"Icing on the cake" benefits you may reap are:

- You respect or like others more as a result of reaching this agreement with them.
- The agreement puts you in a better position than you held before.
- You gain other, unexpected benefits that were not even part of the agreement.

6. You choose consciously how you wish to act and be seen in the world.

Every day, we make conscious or unconscious decisions about how to behave, how to interact with others, and how to present ourselves to the world. Triangle Talk lets you make these decisions consciously.

You take charge of the impression you leave behind, and enhance the quality of your life by developing a stronger sense of who you are and what you are about. Regardless of how others act, you know what your own standards are and can say, "This is how I want to act, *for myself*. This is my commitment to my own integrity and well-being."

EXERCISES

Before we look at Triangle Talk's three steps, take a minute to read through these questions. Use them to pinpoint your "hot spots," to see where you want to improve your conflict-resolving and agreement-reaching skills, and to determine what you would like the Triangle Talk approach to do for you.

- Do you find yourself reacting to what others say or do, rather than setting your own course?
- Have you felt at a disadvantage in forging agreements for yourself in important areas: a job interview, a divorce settlement, a major disagreement with an employer, colleague, or loved one?
- What kinds of people make it difficult for you to communicate effectively? With which kinds of people do you have trouble connecting?
- From whom do you want more understanding or respect?
- When was the last time you were caught off guard and knew you could have done a better job if you'd had more time to prepare?
- Do you sometimes feel awkward "forcing your point" on someone who won't listen?
- Do you have trouble keeping a work group focused on the project at hand, or get irritated when people go off on tangents? Do you know how to bring the group back toward its goal?
- Have you ever wished that people would be clearer about what they want, or that you could read them better?
- Do sales or service people seem to ignore you when you want something?
- Do you feel successful in connecting and communicating at work, but have trouble with the little things at home or with friends?
- Have you ever tried to explain your needs or feelings and had someone respond by saying that he or she felt criticized?

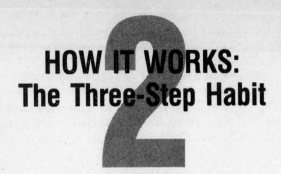

HOW IT WORKS:
The Three-Step Habit

> Once you know that nobody can take from you
> what is really yours, you stop trying to protect it.
> —DR. THEODORA WELLS,
> *Keeping Cool While Under Fire*

Anne collapsed into a chair in my office, letting her purse, briefcase, and several fat file folders fall into a pile on the carpet. We were supposed to discuss a program for the employees at her software company, but that seemed to be the farthest thing from her mind.

"I feel like I'm being pulled in six directions at once," she said. "The people at work need me to do things, my kids need me, my mother needs me . . . I'm always on call, and I'm exhausted. I look good on the outside, but I don't feel like I'm in charge of anything!"

When you're busy and involved with people, it's easy to forget that you're the main character in your own life.

Every human contact involves some kind of negotiation or conflict resolution. You need to make these connections in ways that—

- *Keep you focused* on your own needs and wants but also connected with others and open to what they say.
- *Work as a habit*, so that you don't have to reinvent the wheel with each encounter.

- *Get results* in heated arguments or icy negotiations, major issues or minor spats, when you're tired or feeling great, whether you've seen this discussion coming for years or it sneaks up on you.

Triangle Talk was developed to satisfy exactly these needs. The three steps work together, supporting one another like the legs of a tripod—one of the most solid and stable structures there is. Here is how it works.

Step One: Know Exactly What You Want

To get from Point A to Point B, you have to know where Point B is. Asking "What do I want in this situation?" gives you your exact destination and puts you in the driver's seat. You can direct everything you say and do toward producing that specific result. The more instinctive that question becomes, the more control you have over your own life and the more centered you feel.

For instance, results improve when the sales department moves from a goal of "Increase sales" to "Do $2 million between now and January 1." The members of the sales force have a clear, specific image of what they want and can self-correct if their interim figures aren't heading in that direction.

Similarly, you are more likely to succeed when your goal shifts from "Move up the corporate ladder" to "Become vice-president of marketing within three years."

To know what you want, you have to know who you are and what is important to you. In the course of this book, you will examine your long-term and short-term wants and needs, your self-image and how others see you, your strengths and goals, and what you want to give and receive in various situations and relationships. You will become more aware of the choices you make, and of what you stand for.

Goals that arise from your inherent strengths and profound personal values are stronger and more meaningful. People who can identify and align with their deepest values and goals have a tremendous advantage in life.

Step One keeps you from losing control or getting bogged

down in fear, anger, or hurt. Instead, you can channel all that energy into achieving what you want. Here is how:

If a policeman stops you for speeding, your first reaction might be anger or frustration. You might think, "Why did he have to catch *me*? Doesn't he have anything better to do? Besides, the guy in the red Corvette was going a lot faster! Why didn't he stop *him*?"

That might be your initial response, but as you master Triangle Talk, you will move on quickly to "What do I want in this situation?" Probably, you want not to get a ticket. Flying off the handle is not likely to produce that result. It only gives the officer something to fight against and escalates the conflict. Since he holds all the cards in this particular negotiation, you may be slapped with a second ticket for abusing him.

Step back, calm down, and think about what you want. If you don't want him to give you a ticket, direct your words and actions toward that result. You may be able to cajole, apologize, plead, or reason with him. You may still get a ticket, but at least you stand a chance. If you start screaming abuse at him, you'll get the ticket for sure.

The clearer you are about what you want, the more likely you are to get it. Remember the poster that says, "If you don't know where you're going, you're likely to end up somewhere else."

Step Two: Find Out What They Want and Make Them Feel Heard

After you know what you want, the next step is to find out what the other person wants. You need this information in order to keep moving toward an agreement. It is probably somewhat different from what you want, or the issue would already be resolved.

Those two points—what you want and what the other person wants—form the base of the triangle. You have to know where the other person stands before you can find the third point, the common ground between you.

To find out what others want, you usually have to ask questions. This book gives you highly effective tools for putting other people at ease, encouraging them to open up to you, and discovering what they really want. The most important thing to remember is: *Don't guess, and don't assume. ASK.*

If you are trying to reach an agreement, the question to ask is "What do they want?" If you are arguing, or if they did or said something hurtful, another way to phrase this question is: "Why did they do what they did?" They had a reason, and you can't assume that you know what it is, even if you know them well. (*Be careful*: Don't ask yourself what it would mean if *you* did something; ask what it means when *they* do it.)

The point is to put yourself in their shoes and discover their motivation. The more you know about what they want from this agreement or interaction, the more quickly you can find the common ground and the more effectively you can present your proposal.

The second part of Step Two is to make other people feel heard. They want to know that you have listened and understood what they have said. You don't have to like what they have said, or agree with them; you just have to respect them enough to listen carefully and to acknowledge that you have heard their point of view. You might do this by nodding, repeating or paraphrasing their words, or using phrases like "I understand," "I hear you," or "I see your point of view."

Use language that matters to them. Choose words that reflect their values and their mood. If they have a great respect for thrift, for instance, you might begin, "I can see that we'd save a great deal of money with that plan . . ." If they value honesty, you might say, "I appreciate your being so forthright . . ."

People need their day in the sun, the opportunity to put forth their feelings and ideas without being interrupted or judged, and to know that those feelings and ideas have been heard. If they don't get that kind of attention themselves, they will never give it to you.

Step Three: Propose Action in a Way They Can Accept

The next step is to reach up to the third and highest point of the triangle—the common ground between you. *There is always some area of agreement*, whether or not it appears that

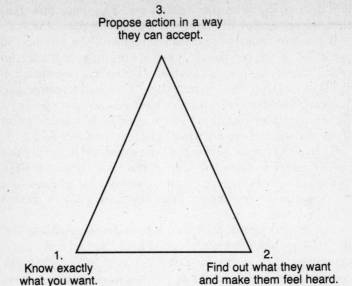

3.
Propose action in a way
they can accept.

1.
Know exactly
what you want.

2.
Find out what they want
and make them feel heard.

way when you first start talking. As you learn more about what you want, and about what the other person wants, that mutual ground becomes clearer. There is almost always a way for both people to win, and to stay connected with one another.

Find a plan that you honestly think can work for both of you, even if you have to bend a little. The point is to achieve your own goals, not to prevent others from achieving theirs. Don't give up what you want, but don't try to steamroll or victimize the other parties. Be fair and reasonable. Don't propose something that insults them. No one wins if you can't reach an agreement, and there is no point in escalating the conflict.

Telling others face to face what you want can be the most challenging part of any negotiation. This book gives you—

- Tools for developing your proposal based on what you want, but characterizing it in terms that appeal to others.
- Techniques for presenting your ideas so that others see them in a favorable light.

- Ways to connect your ideas to the qualities that others admire or value.

If you genuinely want everyone to experience satisfaction, people sense your goodwill. They open up and tell you what they want (even if they don't know what they want when the process begins, Triangle Talk will make them clear on this issue), listen to your ideas, and are more inclined to come to an early, solid agreement.

Remember the triangle and use this visual image to trigger the three steps. The two base points are the foundation that supports your proposal, or common ground.

Triangle Talk in Action

Here is how the three steps worked for one of my clients.

Will was the vice-president in charge of new projects for a developer of regional shopping centers. For six years, he had been trying to contact a man named Kuroski, who owned a large tract of land that Will's company needed for its new development. Kuroski wouldn't answer his letters or return his calls, even though Will had offered a price above market value. When Will went to see him, Kuroski wouldn't even come to the door.

Will was desperate and asked for help from Thomas Jones, a retired executive of his company. Jones took on the project and shepherded the company through the three steps.

First, he met with top executives to make sure they were clear on their primary goal and bottom line. Oddly, there was some confusion when he had them do Step One. When he asked, "What do we really want here?" some people thought they had to have Kuroski's land right away, at any price. Others thought they should consider buying adjacent, less desirable land that was easier to acquire. Others thought the strategy was simply to wait Kuroski out.

Jones repeated an old Chinese saying: "Quieting the chattering mind promotes directed action." He focused the executives' thoughts and asked them to keep narrowing their objective to a primary goal, a vivid mental picture that could be described in one sentence.

Finally, they reached the consensus that they wanted Kuroski's land, but were in no hurry and would sacrifice speed in favor of goodwill from Kuroski and the community, since this would facilitate the local planning review process. Step One was complete.

For Step Two, "Find out what they want and make them feel heard," Jones had to play detective. He drove to the town and checked into the oldest, best established hotel. He went to dinner at the busiest restaurant. In three days, he had informal conversations with nine local people and learned that Kuroski was in his late seventies, the retired owner of a toy company who made regular and generous contributions to local charities.

For the past five years, Kuroski had seldom ventured out of his home. His two children had died in a car accident; his one surviving granddaughter, twenty-three years old, was a kindergarten teacher and advocate of child care for single parents.

Will and others at the company had assumed that Kuroski was just stalling because he had another buyer on the line, but Jones had a different idea. He and Will wrote Kuroski a letter apologizing for their repeated attempts to contact him and asking for just one opportunity to meet. If, after that meeting, Kuroski was not convinced that their shopping center would be of genuine value to the community, they would not attempt to contact him again.

The letter spoke in terms that Kuroski could understand. It mentioned his long history of service to the community; the value of the shopping center in terms of taxes that would support schools, libraries, and other services; their plans to make it reflect the heritage, architecture, and native plantings of the area; and their willingness to offer such innovative services as a community meeting room and low-cost child care.

Kuroski agreed to meet with them, and they found him a sharp-minded man with many questions. He suggested that they consider adding a sporting goods store, which he thought would be of value to the community. He told them that five of the plantings on their list were not actually native to the area and offered substitutes. He asked for written information about their child-care idea, and named a consultant who might work with them to make it cost-effective.

Will and Jones learned that Kuroski was not, in fact, considering another buyer; he simply wasn't accustomed to being hurried. At the end of the meeting, they moved on to Step Three and proposed action in a way that Kuroski could accept.

They said they didn't want to press him to make a decision, but would be available if any questions came up later. They proposed that he sit in on their planning meetings over the next several months to get a sense of the company and its intentions concerning the shopping center. Kuroski became an enthusiastic participant and gave them substantial help with the child-care and landscaping plans.

Three months later, the company told him that it had a tradition of naming centers after community leaders and asked permission to name this one for him if it became a reality. Kuroski said he was honored but would have to think about it. That afternoon, he called and agreed to sell, asking instead that they use only his last name so that the center would be named for his whole family.

Jones had followed the three Triangle Talk steps to turn this stalled negotiation into a successful venture for the company and a living testament to Kuroski's devotion to his community.

First, he insisted that the company executives be very clear and specific about what they wanted, which gave everyone a goal to visualize and a direction in which to move.

Second, he found out what Kuroski really wanted—the profit from the sale wasn't nearly as important to him as making a contribution to the community and the renewed interest in life that he found through working on the project—and then made sure that Kuroski knew they understood and shared his goals.

Jones talked to Kuroski in language that was meaningful to him, and saw the project through the other man's eyes.

Third, he proposed a plan that not only was acceptable to Kuroski because of the goodwill they had built between them, but that made Kuroski an active participant in the development and an enthusiastic member of their team. Again, Jones talked to Kuroski in his own language and did not pressure him to move more quickly than was comfortable for him.

Jones's actions might have seemed manipulative if he had tried to hurry Kuroski, or if he hadn't made good on all his promises along the way. Because Jones's concerns were genuine and his fondness for Kuroski was heartfelt, his actions were taken in the generous spirit in which they were intended.

Triangle Talk gives you a solid base for working through any situation, whether it is more or less important. As you practice the three steps, they become your foundation, the ground from which you start in any negotiation or conflict.

EXERCISES

1. Recall a difficult negotiation or conflict you experienced in the past month.
2. Imagine what might have happened if you had applied the three steps to that situation. What did you really want? What did the other person really want? What was some common ground you found, or might have found?

SIDESTEPPING THE TOP TEN TALK TRAPS

In many cases stress is caused not by the event itself but rather our response to the event.
—Dr. Robert Eliot, author of
Is It Worth Dying For?

What goes wrong when conflicts fly out of control, talks break down, agreements can't be reached, or negotiations stall? The trouble usually starts when one of the three steps is forgotten or avoided.

Triangle Talk lets you take charge of these potential disasters and manage events so that everyone feels positive about the result.

Pressure Points

Whenever your life touches another person's, some kind of agreement is reached or conflict resolved—even if it is only about who, if anyone, will smile first. Whether the other person is your CEO or the hotel reservations clerk, there is an opportunity for either positive results or stress and conflict. It may mean a quantum leap in your career, or simply a pleasant welcome to the hotel. It may mean jeopardizing your job, or merely a brief struggle over getting a room with a view.

In either case, it's to your advantage to have some influence over the outcome.

Since everyone wants these exchanges and agreements to work, why do they so often fail? Why do people stop talking, and either start fighting or go away? Why do so many people say things like:

- "I think I know what I want, but people tune out when I start talking about it."
- "I don't know what's the matter with the people who work for me. I tell them a million times what to do, but they never get it right."
- "I'm okay with anyone except Eleanor. She walks into the room and I go nuts."
- "It always seems like someone has to be the winner and someone has to be the loser. Unless I steamroll the other person, I can't have what I want."
- "I lose it when I'm put on the spot and have to give an answer quickly."

The Top Ten Talk Traps

These people have fallen into communication traps that make it difficult to resolve conflicts or reach agreements, and often lead either to screaming or to stony silence. Knowing where the pitfalls are makes it easier to avoid them.

The top ten talk traps are the following:

1. Me First

Karen was a free-lance artist who wanted to illustrate a series of nature texts. She went into the interview determined to impress Jack, who was in charge of hiring an artist for the project. After spreading her portfolio all over his desk, she sat down and talked nonstop for twenty minutes—about herself.

She was vaguely aware of Jack slipping deeper into his chair and studying a spot on the wall, but didn't know what to do and continued for another five minutes about her past successes, the quality of her work, and what she had in mind for the nature series.

She never asked Jack about the series or what he envisioned for it. In fact, she didn't ask any questions at all. Jack liked her work very much, but was put off by her overbearing manner and the fact that she seemed much more interested in herself than in him, his company, his ideas, or even the series.

He also saw that she misunderstood what they intended to do with the series and was taking it in a whole different direction. He wasn't sure she even wanted to hear their ideas; he worried that it might be hard to keep her on track, and he didn't want to risk working with someone who couldn't take direction.

Karen was surprised when she didn't get the job. Jack told a colleague, "I was disappointed we couldn't use her because she's a terrific artist, but she didn't seem at all interested in our ideas and it didn't look like she'd fit in on the team."

Karen had done Step One and knew what she wanted—to do the artwork for the nature series—but she completely ignored Step Two. She never even bothered to find out what Jack wanted, let alone make him feel heard.

Even if Karen had realized after twenty minutes what was happening, it might have been too late. People listen better, sooner, and longer when you speak to *their* needs first. When you speak to your own needs before theirs, it often creates a negative first impression that's hard to overcome. Asking questions too late can remind people of the old line, "But enough about me . . . what do *you* think about me?"

Research shows that people speak first to the other person's needs only 3 percent of the time. This figure helps explain why negotiations break down so often and suggests the advantage of being part of that wise and effective 3 percent.

We usually speak first to our own needs because we are unclear about what we want and are trying to figure it out as we talk, or because we're secretly afraid we can't have it and we are trying to trick, overwhelm, or fast-talk others into giving it to us. The result is that people close down and are less receptive to what we say.

Triangle Talk avoids this trap because—

- Step One makes you confident about your own goals, so that you avoid any uncertainty or insecurity that might prompt you to speak first to your own needs.
- You don't propose solutions (Step Three) until you've found out what others want and made them feel heard (Step Two). You have to ask them about themselves and their ideas in order to establish the second base point of the triangle. Only then can you move on to the third point, which is your common ground.
- You know what you want, so you don't sit there pretending to listen to them, but actually trying to figure out your own needs. They know you've heard what they said because you really *have*.

2. *You First*

Dorothy presented a three-day course in management to executives across the United States and Canada on behalf of a national management consulting firm. The course was standardized, with only minor adjustments for each corporation, and Dorothy used the same set of support tools—overhead projector, flip charts, blackboard, etc.—wherever she went.

It was going to be very complicated to get all this equipment to Uniflo's executive retreat at a rustic inn three and a half hours outside Vancouver. Burt, who was Dorothy's contact at Uniflo, said, "Oh, don't worry about hauling all that stuff up here. Just tell me what you need and I'll make sure it's at the inn when we arrive. It'll be much easier for everyone that way."

Dorothy wasn't entirely comfortable with this, but she didn't want to be unpleasant or suggest to Burt that she didn't trust him. She hesitated a moment, then agreed to let him handle it.

When she arrived at the inn, there was no flip chart or blackboard, and the overhead projector wasn't the kind she needed. Dorothy was furious with Burt and told her cofacilitator, "I knew he'd make a mess of this and undermine the program."

Dorothy never completed Step One. She was so afraid of not being nice that she didn't let herself explore what she really wanted in this situation.

If she had, she probably would have come up with something like "I want my firm to make whatever shipping arrangements are necessary to get that equipment to the inn three days before we arrive—even if it has to be dragged in by dogsled. Then I want to send a detailed inventory of what should be included to someone at the inn, have that person check it, and call me to confirm that everything arrived."

It's not fair to blame others for the result when you don't take the time, or muster up the courage, to be clear about what you want—and then let them know what it is.

You *speak* first to others' needs when you use Triangle Talk, but you *think* first about your own. This keeps you from getting stuck in the "You First" trap.

3. Emotional Overload

Barbara and Carl were partners in a medical practice as well as marriage partners. After their divorce, which went relatively well but was nevertheless painful for both, they decided to bite the bullet and force themselves to get along because they had both worked so hard to build their practice and it was quite successful.

This worked well for a few months, but then Carl started to donate a great deal of his time at a free clinic, which put a significant financial strain on the practice. Barbara pointed this out to him, but Carl just ignored her and seemed to do even more work at the clinic.

One morning after a meeting with their accountant, she flew into a rage. "You're going to wreck this practice, just like you wrecked our marriage!" she screamed.

"You're a selfish bitch. If you cared about anybody except yourself, we'd still have a marriage!" he countered.

"*Someone* has to be practical and take care of business. We'd starve if it were up to you," she yelled.

The discussion escalated until finally Carl said, "If you're so good at taking care of things, it's all yours. I quit."

It is far more difficult to resolve conflicts or reach agreements with people for whom we have strong feelings—love or hate—than with people toward whom we feel neutral. The stakes are higher with these people, our "scripts" are already in place, we may not think as clearly, and we're inclined to go "on automatic."

Triangle Talk helps you steer clear of this trap in Step One by shifting the energy and attention from feelings to facts, from "How do I *feel?*" to "What do I *want?*" This doesn't make all the discomfort evaporate immediately, but it points you toward solid ground where difficulties *can* be worked out.

4. Surprise!

Allen was famous at his law firm for working out difficult contracts. He was the ace who always brought in the most important clients, and he dazzled people with his expertise even though he had only come to work for the firm a few months earlier.

They had not yet discovered that, although Allen was a near-genius when he had plenty of time to prepare, he didn't think on his feet very well. When the firm's top client needed a contract resolved by three o'clock one afternoon, Allen was the natural choice.

At one, he sat down with the other party's attorney despite a churning stomach, a dry mouth, a tendency to forget the details of the case, and a feeling of panic. By two-thirty, he had given away the shirt off his client's back.

Caught off guard without time to plan, even the best problem-solvers can freeze up, forget important points, or say inappropriate and unproductive things that catapult the situation from bad to worse.

If Allen had used the Triangle Talk approach, his first response—even when he was caught off guard—would have been Step One, "What do I want?" That would have focused his attention and the discussion on what would benefit his client. Those goals would have become the point of departure for everything he said and did. With the image of the triangle in his mind, he could have worked through the three steps and might have saved his deal.

5. But It Worked Last Time . . .

Ted had just opened his own small public relations firm and was learning quickly how to deal with difficult clients.

When Ajax Chemicals threatened to pull its business and hire a competitive firm, Ted took the Ajax president out for a fancy steak dinner and made the effort to establish a strong personal connection. They both had teenage children and shared many political views. The tactic worked; Ajax stopped talking about leaving.

When the director of St. Rita's Hospital criticized the way Ted had handled the publicity for the hospital's spring benefit, Ted smugly asked the director to dinner at the same steakhouse. This man also had teenage children, but didn't care at all for Ted's approach and said, "I find this evening unprofessional and offensive. Don't think you can make up for poor performance by wining and dining me. We'll be changing our account to someone who can concentrate on his work."

What works in one situation may be disastrous in another.

Ted knew what he wanted—to keep St. Rita's as a client—but he forgot Step Two. He never found out exactly what the director's problems were and what he wanted, and he didn't make the director feel heard. Ted just went forward with his own agenda without bothering to listen or speak to the director's specific, individual needs . . . and it lost him the client.

6. Bullying

Don ran the auto body shop where Carol took her car after an accident to have the passenger door undented and repainted. He gave her a written estimate of $350 and scheduled an appointment.

Carol brought the car in the next Thursday morning at seven-thirty, then rode the bus for forty-five minutes to work. When she arrived, she found a message from Don saying that he'd forgotten to include the cost of the paint in his estimate and that the job would cost an additional $90.

Don's business had been slow and he was trying a tactic that another body shop owner had suggested to him. His friend had told him that people usually just grumbled and let him go ahead with the work at the higher cost. They didn't want to take a bus or cab down to the shop again to pick up their cars when they'd already gotten up early and made arrangements to be without their vehicles for the day.

This tactic didn't work with Carol. She said she had a written estimate of $350 and that he was obliged to honor that. Don said that there was nothing he could do, that he had to pay for the paint, and that the job would now cost $440 or he wouldn't do it. In a further attempt to intimidate her, he yelled, "Look, it'll cost you that much anywhere. Don't be stupid. What're you gonna do, take more time off and come down here to grab your car?"

That was exactly what she did. Then she wrote a letter about the incident to the Better Business Bureau, enclosed a copy of Don's written estimate, and sent another copy to the insurance companies and car dealerships that regularly recommended Don's shop. His business got even slower.

People know when they are being manipulated or bullied, and their reaction is usually to resist, shut down, withdraw, fight back, and possibly never trust you again.

Don made a mistake by trying to bully Carol in the first place, but he could have saved the situation by making her feel heard and just letting her come to pick up the car (Step Two) instead of screaming at her and trying to force the issue over the phone. If he had come clean and apologized, she might still have taken her car to another body shop, but she probably wouldn't have written those letters.

7. You Can't Get There from Here

Daniel had just completed a medical internship and didn't know what he wanted to do next when he got a call from Dr. Williams, an older physician in St. Louis, inviting him to come and "talk about your future, perhaps about going into practice together." Dr. Williams had a friend who had been one of Daniel's teachers in medical school and had recommended him in glowing terms.

Daniel arrived at the office, sat down, and smiled at Dr. Williams, who smiled back. "So, tell me about yourself," Dr.

Williams began. Daniel had no idea whether he even wanted to go into private practice, didn't want to make any commitments, and didn't want to embarrass his former teacher by making a mistake, so he gave a sketchy, minimal, lackluster description of medical school and his recent internship.

Dr. Williams was unimpressed, but kept trying to draw Daniel out on the basis of his friend's recommendation. Daniel didn't know what to say, so he said very little. He kept waiting for clues from Dr. Williams, but got none.

Dr. Williams kept waiting for clues from Daniel, because he didn't know what he wanted either. He hadn't even thought about taking on a partner until his old friend had called, and still didn't know how he felt about it. He was waiting to see what kind of a guy Daniel was, and what he had to say for himself.

After forty minutes, Daniel couldn't imagine what had possessed him to come to St. Louis, and wished he were on the moon. After an hour, both men were exhausted and gave up, having accomplished nothing.

When you don't know what you want, you can't direct the discussion toward your goals and may wind up talking in circles. Nobody gets what he or she wants, and you feel as though you've been run over by a truck.

Both Daniel and Dr. Williams ignored Steps One and Two. Neither was exactly sure what he wanted from the situation, and neither bothered to find out specifically what the other wanted. Since both were missing the triangle's two base points, it's no wonder that they never talked about Step Three, the common ground and solutions.

8. Blind Man's Buff

Fran and Joe had saved their money to start a bed-and-breakfast in the country when they retired. As that day approached, they were still arguing about where to buy this quaint little place. Fran wanted to go "to the beach, to the lake . . . I don't even have to swim; I just want to be able to look out at the water." Joe wanted the mountains, and said they might as well stay in the city if he couldn't ski.

They fought tooth and nail, each attacking the other's preference and both becoming so entrenched in their positions that the conflict turned into a death struggle—the death of their cherished project. They finally resigned themselves to buying a bed-and-breakfast in the city, and neither of them was truly happy.

They were so consumed by their argument, so insistent that the other person *not win*, that they never even thought of buying near Lake Tahoe—a lake in the mountains which would have satisfied both of their needs, and which also had a flourishing tourist industry.

We can be so determined to get our own needs met, or to tear down other people's needs if they seem to conflict with ours, that we never even look for the common ground that would please us both.

Joe and Fran completed Step One and part of Step Two, but then they stopped dead in their tracks. Step Two isn't finding out what others want and resisting it to the death. It's about getting behind their eyes (at least for a moment), seeing things as they do, and then letting them know that you hear what they are saying.

Joe and Fran never moved on to Step Three, the common ground, because they never finished Step Two. They never took the time and energy to get behind one another's eyes and make one another feel heard.

9. Speeding

Robin was the fast-talking property manager in charge of keeping a downtown office building rented, and he was almost positive that he could get Dyna-Tech's signature on a lease for the third-floor suite that afternoon if he played his cards right.

When Dyna-Tech's vice-president and office manager came to look at the space, Robin swept them through the offices in about five minutes and had them back in the reception area with the lease on the table before they'd even taken off their coats.

They hadn't raised any questions, so he figured everything was going smoothly or, as he was fond of saying, "like a hot knife through butter."

They had no sooner sat down than he shoved the lease under their noses and held out a pen. The vice-president looked at the office manager. The office manager looked at the vice-president. They stood as one person, tersely thanked Robin for his time, walked out the door, and were never seen again.

"Go slow to go fast later" is an important part of Triangle Talk, especially when you are doing Step Two: Find out what people want and make them feel heard. You can't just go through the motions. You can't ask people once, and then push them ahead if they don't have much to say. You really do have to find out what they want, even if it takes a little time.

If you try to hurry people through the three steps, the negotiation is more likely to blow up at the last minute and you may never reach the agreement.

10. But I Assumed . . .

Brad was one of three contractors bidding on a condominium complex for a local developer. He hadn't bothered to find out much about the developer and assumed that everyone thought faster construction was better. Based on this assumption, he figured out the absolute minimum time it would take him to finish the project and used that completion date in the bid.

The three bids were about equal in terms of cost, but Brad's time estimate was considerably shorter than the other two. The developer figured that either he didn't know what he was talking about, or he intended to cut corners and do slipshod work. Time wasn't nearly as important to the developer as doing things well and at a minimal cost, so he eliminated Brad immediately.

You will never fall into this trap if you do Step Two. You'll know exactly what the other person wants and will be able to speak to those needs as you negotiate. You'll have the second base point of the triangle firmly in place, and will know where to look for the third point or common ground.

The three steps of Triangle Talk let you deal in reality, rather than in fears, hopes, or illusions. You know exactly what you want, what others want, and where your common ground lies. This gives you more control in any situation; it helps you avoid these and other talk traps, and puts you in charge of your circumstances and your life.

EXERCISES

1. Think of a situation that was not resolved to your satisfaction.
2. Which of these ten talk traps was operating, or which of the three steps wasn't implemented fully?
3. What could you have done to resolve the situation in a mutually satisfying way?
4. Which of these talk traps do you find yourself in most often? Which do you usually manage to avoid?

STEP ONE:
Know Exactly What You Want

KNOW YOUR BOTTOM LINE: The "What Do I Want?" Habit

> Defining yourself and your options gives you choices. As you fix the problem, you won't need to fix the blame.
>
> —DR. THEODORA WELLS

The first, most basic step in any attempt to reach agreement is knowing exactly what you want. The next two chapters give specific techniques for discovering and staying focused on what you want—in the short term and the long.

Step One: Know Exactly What You Want

Step One is simple. Whenever you feel confused, angry, hurt, muddled, steamrolled, stymied, stonewalled, stalemated, or at any kind of disadvantage, you only have to ask one thing: "What do I want?" This question focuses your thoughts and starts you moving through the three steps.

Bill waited until just a few minutes before the meeting with an important client to tell Jessie that he'd given the promotion (and substantial raise) she'd been expecting to a man who had been at the company half as long as she had—and who she felt was half as competent as she was. When her jaw dropped, Bill tried to jolly her out of the shock and said, "Hey, he has a family to support. He does a good job. What could I do?"

Jessie's first impulse was to lash out at Bill—physically and verbally—for treating her so unfairly. The blood rose in her face. She wanted to scream at him, walk out and leave him to deal with the client, break everything she could get her hands on as she marched out of the building, and slap the company with a crippling lawsuit.

That helpless, out-of-control, "I want to break something" feeling was a signal to her. She had practiced the Triangle Talk habit enough to know when it was time to stop operating on instincts that might get her into deeper trouble, and start with Step One.

She forced herself to calm down and ask, "What do I really want here?" One thing she did *not* want was for people to think she was a hysterical woman who ran out of buildings screaming and breaking things.

Three possibilities flashed through her mind:

1. She might still get the promotion, or at least the raise —either by gently persuading them to do the right thing, or by threatening to sue them blind.
2. She could sue, win, and retire comfortably at thirty-five.
3. At the least, she wanted to be sure she kept her present job until she found another one.

None of these options would be served by flying off the handle with Bill and appearing to be incompetent, out of control, or a saboteur right before the important meeting. What she wanted right then, in that moment, was to be cool and collected, to get through the day, and to give herself some time to react and consider her options when she got home.

She looked Bill in the eye, gave him a brief, confident smile, and started going over the details of their meeting with the client. He was shaken by her lack of reaction, and appeared in her office late that afternoon offering perks and concessions. Jessie remained aloof and said, "I think we all need some time to think this over, Bill. Why don't you and I get together at the end of the week to figure out what we're going to do."

In this particular case, Jessie held all the legal cards—it was a clear case of discrimination, as her lawyer pointed out the next afternoon—but she could have thrown them away if she hadn't stopped her emotional outburst and grounded herself with "What do I want?"

Knowing what you want gives you a foundation, a purpose, and a driving force for everything you do. You have a context, a framework in which to monitor the situation as it unfolds. It's easier to remember what is important and what is not, so you are more open and flexible, better able to listen to others. When you understand your bottom line, all the other pieces are more likely to fall into place.

The Cornerstone Question: "What Do I Want?"

Asking "What do I want?" gives you three major benefits:

1. You are more in control and feel more relaxed. If you know what you want before you go into a situation or meeting, you will probably feel more confident. You'll be less rigid in your demands and will set an open, relaxed tone that also helps others be more comfortable and flexible.

When you *don't* know what you want, it's easy to feel defensive and combative—to compensate for the uncertainty by "digging in" and refusing to budge.

Jack and Ed's excellent customer service had made their San Francisco computer hardware business so successful that they had decided to open another store. They had researched several sites and narrowed the choice to Berkeley or San Rafael. Jack had always favored San Rafael, but Ed hadn't made up his mind.

When they met to make the final decision, Jack sat down and put forth his rationale for choosing San Rafael. Ed wasn't sold on Berkeley, but he wasn't about to be railroaded. He tried to punch holes in Jack's arguments, made a case against San Rafael rather than for Berkeley, and snapped back negative reactions to everything Jack said.

Jack was secure in knowing what he wanted, so he didn't feel the need to fire back. He simply waited Ed out, listening to his tirades and letting Ed know that he saw his point of view. Finally, Ed ran out of steam and realized that San Rafael was actually a better business decision. He saw that his opposition had been based more on feeling defensive and uncertain than on not wanting the second store to be in San Rafael.

The venture was ultimately a success, but Ed's uncertainty had made the process more difficult and unpleasant than it might have been.

2. *You keep focused on specific goals that mean something to you.* Asking "What do I want?" fine-tunes your internal TV screen. What was fuzzy becomes clear. What was distorted comes into perspective. Whether your bottom line is a dollar amount, the picture of a perfect job, or the conditions of a contract, you know exactly where you are and where you're going. You know when you have it and when you don't, so you can self-correct if necessary.

When you've asked "What do I want in life?" as well as "What do I want in this situation?" your smaller goals emerge out of this larger vision. You see the forest *and* the trees. Your whole life takes on a harmony, clarity, and internal integrity that feel great and give you a powerful position from which to enter the world.

Alice learned an important lesson the first time she bid a job for her new landscaping business. A couple who had just bought their first house and wanted a backyard garden were considering several landscapers, and Alice absolutely refused to be underbid. She had a vague idea of how much the plants, irrigation system, and labor would cost, but she didn't want any of these amounts set in stone. She was prepared to bid as low as necessary to get the work, and she sat down with the couple without any firm figures in mind.

They had no idea how much these things cost, but they sensed her uncertainty and talked her down to a ridiculously low price. It cost Alice hundreds of dollars to do that job.

Not only had she sabotaged herself by going into the meeting without knowing exactly what she wanted, but she had forgotten to look at the forest as well as the trees. She hadn't considered the big picture of which that job was only a small part.

Alice had started her landscaping business because she loved working outdoors with plants and wanted to be her own boss. To make that dream a reality, the business had to make money. It wouldn't do Alice any good to be outdoors working with plants if she couldn't eat, so she sat down and figured out what percentage of profit she had to show on each job for the business to succeed—and she never went into another meeting without a complete command of the costs, a specific bid, and a bottom line beyond which she absolutely would not go.

Alice learned to give her own needs the same importance that she gave others' needs, and to remember her long-term objective—having a successful business—as well as her short-term goal of landing individual jobs.

3. You shift the attention from emotions *to* issues, *from* feelings *to* facts, *from* ego *to an* action plan. This keeps you from getting caught up in knee-jerk negative emotional reactions that escalate the conflict and rob you of your ability to negotiate effectively.

We are trained to respond to conflict or disagreement by asking ourselves, "What are they doing to me and how do I feel about it?" This question puts you on the defensive and moves the problem into emotional quicksand. How you feel, what you do, and the direction you take are all determined by other people. You are likely to feel out of control, beaten up, and not heard or respected. The more you concentrate on how you feel, the more strongly you will feel those negative emotions and the more likely you are to escalate the conflict, rather than choosing your course of action. This path produces no positive results; it is simply a waste of time and energy.

The more productive question is "What do I want in this situation?" This shifts your attention, and other people's attention, away from negative emotional reactions and back to the issues at hand. It gives you something concrete to talk about and work toward. You now have an arena in which results can be produced.

You may have to retrain yourself to ask this question, and work on developing the new habit.

Avoid Asking:
- "Who's right?"
- "What are they doing to me?"
- "How do I feel about it?"

Do Ask:
- "What do I want?"
- "What is the result that's most important to me here?"
- "If I had complete control over this situation, what would I want to happen?"

These are the real issues, the things you can control. Being clear about what you want keeps you calm, steady, and moving toward your goals—even when you are around difficult people who press your "hot buttons" or when everyone else is going crazy. In fact, your concentration on "What do I want?" rather than "How do I feel?" makes it easier for others to calm down and get focused as well.

Jim was a middle manager at a construction company that was experiencing rough times, and he was asked to take a cut in pay. He and his wife, Jan, were struggling to pay the mortgage and keep their two children in good schools. He had actually been planning to ask for a raise, and the request to take a salary cut threw him into a tailspin.

He felt angry, resentful, depressed, and unappreciated. He couldn't help thinking that they were cutting his salary because they didn't like his work, even though he knew that wasn't true.

After a week of wallowing in these negative emotions, he and Jan sat down and asked, "What do we want?" Jim considered leaving the company, but decided he'd rather stay and ride out the hard times if it could give him enough for the family to live on.

He and Jan worked out the minimum that he needed to bring home each month. Since this was more than he would make with the salary cut, Jim considered what additional responsibilities he could take on in order to bring his salary up to that amount. Now he knew his bottom line. He scheduled a meeting with his boss.

At the meeting, all Jim's anger rose to the surface again. He was surprised that his boss seemed defensive and angry as well, until he realized that the boss probably wasn't enjoying this process, either. She was having to cut people's salaries and probably getting some unpleasant reactions.

Jim didn't let his own feelings put a negative cast on their conversation. Instead, he remembered the image of the triangle and focused on the issues, not his emotions. He took control of the situation by concentrating on what he wanted. When he calmed down and zeroed in on the issues, his boss seemed to relax as well.

Jim took out the list that he and Jan had prepared and made his proposal. The boss was impressed, and the two of them started figuring out what new work he could take on so that the company could afford to keep him. By concentrating on the facts, rather than their feelings about one another, Jim and his boss came to an agreement. The added benefit was that they liked and respected one another more.

Step One doesn't mean that you can't have emotional reactions when terrible things happen or people treat you badly. You can, and it's important to find an environment where you can release those emotions freely and safely. The Step One shift from feelings to facts, from emotions to issues, simply lets you choose when and where you bring those emotions to the surface, so that you don't jeopardize your future, escalate the conflict unnecessarily, lose relationships, or walk away when you need to stand your ground.

As we discuss each of the three steps, the 100 techniques that make them work faster and better will be highlighted. These techniques are also listed alone for quick review in "The Fast Track" at the end of this book.

TECHNIQUE #1:
Make "What Do I Want?" an Automatic Response

When you learn to make "What do I want?" an instinctive response to daily situations, life becomes far less stressful and confusing. Challenging situations will always arise—that's part of life—but you never have to be thrown off center or caught off guard in a situation you don't think you can handle. Whenever the circumstances feel fuzzy, uncertain, or unsettling, develop the habit of asking yourself immediately, "What do I want?"

Pat's first job was as a reporter for a small daily newspaper in Indiana. On any given day, she might be sent to cover a city council meeting, a zoning board session, and a birth at the local zoo. She was constantly meeting new people and having to extract accurate, detailed information from them.

Then she had to rush back to the city room and write up the stories under the scrutiny of her tough, cigar-smoking, *Front Page*-style editor, follow up on anything that he thought was unclear, and nail everything down before the deadline.

"Sometimes I even forgot which meeting I was at," she said. "I'd have to look at the sign on the desk or glance around the room to see where I was. Talk about the need to be centered! 'What do I want?' saved my life. When I felt myself drifting, I'd just say, 'What do I want?' Then I'd answer, 'To find out these five things: . . .' When politicians gave me trouble, instead of tossing back a smart remark, I'd say, 'What do I want?' and come up with 'The real answer to that question I asked.'

"Back at my desk, with all the stories whirling around in my mind, I'd ask the question and choose one thing, like 'To get the zoning commission piece done by eleven o'clock.' That gave me a mental picture to concentrate on. It kept my mind from shooting off in a million directions."

The habit of asking "What do I want?" can be especially useful during a conflict or argument. It changes the problem from a struggle between egos to a difference between goals and points of view. Even if only one person—you—makes this shift, the energy changes and the tension begins to lift. You put the discussion back on ground that can yield positive results. There is almost always something that you want more than you want the fight or the emotional outburst.

Lori was in the unfortunate position of doing secretarial work for three people. None of her bosses knew how much work the others had given her, and Lori often felt that she was doing the work of three people but only getting one-third of the credit she deserved.

One of these bosses was in the habit of sauntering by, dropping a file folder on her desk from about a foot up, and asking contemptuously, "Any reason you can't have that done by tomorrow morning?"

One day when he did this, Lori saw red. She was just about to fly off the handle, possibly jeopardizing her job, when she remembered to ask, "What do I want?" Her answer was that she wanted all the bosses to know what she was doing, so that they wouldn't make unreasonable demands of her. She also wanted them to know why she couldn't always drop everything and do what they asked.

Lori devised a system that would produce this result. She divided a board above her desk into three columns and put one boss's name at the top of each one. Then she wrote the name of each task or project on a Post-it note and put it in the appropriate column. When the bosses came by with work for her, she pointedly consulted her board. They could see for themselves how busy she was and where their projects stood in the waiting line. Sometimes she had to say, "I'll get to it as quickly as I can, but as you can see, there's a lot of work scheduled before it."

By asking "What do I want?" Lori turned what could have been a disaster into a significant improvement in her working conditions.

When you first start to develop the "What do I want?" habit, it may seem that you are asking yourself that question hundreds of times a day—and you may be doing just that! It can feel awkward at first, because we are not taught to ask that question or to think in those terms. Stay with it and practice until the habit is second nature. It will focus your entire life and give you tremendous clarity and peace of mind.

TECHNIQUE #2:
Decide What You Want by Considering Alternatives, Then Choosing One

Some people have difficulty deciding what they want, in specific situations and in life. Often this is because they are thinking in terms that are too general. They want to be "happy" or "rich" or "fulfilled." They don't think in specifics like "Make $40,000 a year" or "Be content that I've done my best at the end of each day."

If you are having trouble deciding what you want in any given situation, try thinking in more concrete terms. Write down some specific possibilities and alternatives. They may not be exactly what you want, or even reasonable choices, but they will start your mind working on the problem and prompt other thoughts and possibilities.

Rick was a real estate agent and had complained for years about the ups and downs of the industry in Texas. When the bottom dropped out of the market again, he decided to get out of the field for good. He was forty-one, had a B.A. in history, and didn't know where to start looking for a new career.

After the initial wave of fear and depression—Did he have any marketable skills, other than selling? Who would want him at this age? How could he start over after all these years?—he sat down with a thick pad of paper and started to write.

Rick made lists of things he could do, things he liked to do, things he'd dreamed of doing, and things he thought he might be able to do. He talked to a career counselor who gave him encouragement, guidance, and ideas for more lists. Eventually, he honed all his lists down to one titled "Jobs I'm Considering," with three items on it:

1. Stay in real estate and move to Seattle.
2. Sell medical supplies.
3. Start a house-painting business.

That was a manageable decision, something he could get his mind around and tackle objectively. He was no longer bobbing around in a sea of generalities and uncertainties—vacillating, fearful, and exhausted just from thinking about the future. He had a rational choice among three items, and picked selling medical supplies. Going through that process gave Rick a confidence that he projected to potential employers, and he had a new job within three months.

TECHNIQUE #3:
Create a Specific, Vivid Mental Image of What You Want and Describe It in One Sentence

Be specific about what you want, and create a vivid mental picture of the result. An effective bottom line is a precise, striking mental image that you can express in one sentence.

The technique of visualizing goals enjoys wide acceptance and enthusiasm in business, sports, and many other fields. Experts agree that the more specific and vivid you make your mental picture, the more effective it is. Exactly what would your result look like? How would it make you feel? Fill in as many details as you can, and involve as many physical senses as possible (sight, sound, touch, taste, and smell).

Too vague: "I want things to go my way in the meeting."
More specific: "I want her signature on this contract."

Too vague: "I want him to be more cooperative."
More specific: "I want him to have those time sheets on my desk by nine o'clock each Monday morning."

A child says, "I want your cup." An adult says, "I want your stuff." The older we get, the more abstract our thinking becomes—and the more we have to discipline ourselves to be specific.

Don was director of sales for a new Chicago hotel and wanted to book a farm association's annual convention. The convention's representative, Owen Rider, was coming to town to look at the facilities and have lunch in the hotel dining room.

Don was very clear about what he wanted—the farm association's business—but he took it a step further. For about a week before Owen came to town, Don spent a few moments each day thinking about how he wanted their meeting to go and creating a vivid mental picture of its success.

He imagined Owen coming through the beautifully decorated hotel lobby and thinking what a pleasant place the hotel was. He pictured Owen walking into his office and the two of them shaking hands, then followed himself and Owen around as they toured the meeting facilities and guest rooms.

Don knew that the more physical senses he could involve in his picture, the more powerful it would be. When he saw himself and Owen sitting down to lunch, he imagined the smell of wonderful food floating through the dining room, the bright twinkling of chandeliers above them, and the taste of a delicious meal in his mouth.

He imagined telling Owen about all the features and benefits that the association could expect if it chose his hotel for the convention, and finally created a picture of Owen smiling, accepting, and reaching out to shake his hand.

Don knew that mental imagery was powerful, but was still a bit startled when events unrolled almost exactly as he had pictured them.

Knowing what you want before you go into a situation is the foundation of success. Asking what you want in the midst of conflict is your ticket to sanity and to achieving your goals. Step One gives you a context, a focus, and a point of reference for everything else you do.

EXERCISES

1. Write down a situation that is currently troubling you or about which you feel unclear or uncertain.
2. Apply the question "What do I want?"
3. Write down what you really want in that situation, and what you must do to get it.

KNOW YOURSELF:
What Do You Stand For?

The only person I control in the entire world is me.
People work in their own best interests, not mine.
It used to be that my people were responsible to
me. Now I am responsible to them.

—RALPH STAYER,
principal owner, Johnsonville Foods,
Sheboygan Falls, Wisconsin

Step One—Know exactly what you want—is about making choices. The better you know yourself, the better choices you will make.

Choices that are based on genuine beliefs and values—what is truly important to you in life—keep you centered and make life a more exciting, fulfilling enterprise. When you know who you are, what you stand for, and what you value most, you can make authentic, powerful choices that have the weight of your conviction and commitment behind them.

TECHNIQUE #4:
Understand What Is Most Important to You

Most people don't take the time to sit down regularly and reexamine what is truly important to them. They assume they already know, or they just don't think about it because there are so many things they *have* to do each day, or they plan to take time out to look "later," or "someday, when the dust settles."

Knowing what you want *today*—not what you may have wanted at some other time in your life—is an invaluable asset. These are some questions you can ask to determine what is important to you now:

What Is Important?
- What do I value most in life?
- For what do I want to be remembered?
- What makes me happiest?
- What gives me the most satisfaction and sense of fulfillment?
- What has seemed most important to me in the past five years?
- What is actually most important to me now?
- What are the ten most important things in my life?

Who Is Important?
- Who are the five most important people to me?
- What impact does each of these people have on my life?

What Are My Goals?
- What are my top three one-year professional goals?
- What are my top three one-year personal goals?
- What are the similarities and conflicts between them?
- What are my top three five-year professional goals?
- What are my top three five-year personal goals?
- What are the similarities and conflicts between them?

Values change as we grow and evolve. Take time at least once a year to stay current on what is important to you.

TECHNIQUE #5:
Develop a "Larger Than Life" Vision of Yourself, Your Work, and Your Life

It's easy to get caught up in routine and forget that you are bigger than any one task or any day's "to do" list. You need a vision of yourself and your life that goes beyond everyday necessities and gives you a bigger purpose.

Having a larger vision makes all your smaller decisions easier and more consistent. Everything you do is guided by this larger sense of purpose and direction. Your life goals determine your career, your career goals determine your job, your job goals determine what you do this morning, and so on.

A "larger than life" vision of yourself, your work, and your life might be: "What's most important to me are connections with people, and the way that shows up in my life is through my family." Some of the specific goals that might help you fulfill that vision are—

1. Earning enough to support the family comfortably.
2. Making sure you take at least two weeks off each year for a family vacation or activities.
3. Not giving in to workaholic tendencies and making sure you spend time with the children each night.

Another "larger than life" vision might be world peace. Someone with this vision might work for an organization that supports world peace, or share activities promoting world peace with family and friends.

Any "larger than life" vision involves more than just your own individual life. It comes from your best, most altruistic self, and can be the light that guides you through difficult or uncertain times.

A larger vision not only enriches your life, it also inspires interest, trust, and loyalty in others. You become a more effective natural leader.

Answer these questions to discover your own "larger than life" vision:

- What do I want to stand for in my work? Is this answer the same as what my company stands for?
- What do I stand for in my personal life?
- What is consistent between what I want to stand for in work and what I stand for in my personal life?
- Are there any conflicts?
- What can I do about them?

- What can I do today, and in the next few weeks, to make my life more consistent with my "larger than life" vision?

TECHNIQUE #6:
Know How You See Yourself, and How Others See You

Joel was a brilliant, considerate, attractive man, but he was shy and thought of himself as socially inept—so he never made a strong impression. Who you *think* you are can be as important as who you are.

Understand the way you see yourself and check these assumptions against reality so that they don't limit you.

Find out how others see you and ask yourself if this is how you want to be seen. Are others' assumptions about you helping you get what you want, or holding you back?

Use these questions to start examining your self-image and the image that others have of you. You may want to get a friend or colleague's input on the questions that deal with how others see you.

- What are the first six adjectives that you would use to describe yourself?
- What are the first six adjectives you think others would use to describe you?
- What do you consider your six greatest strengths and weaknesses?
- What do you think others consider your six greatest strengths and weaknesses?
- Are you a task-oriented person or a people-oriented person?
- How do others see you—as task-oriented or people-oriented?
- Are you inclined to be highly expressive and dramatic (high affect) or are you more shy, reserved, and noncommittal (low affect)?
- Do others perceive you in the same way?

- What is your instinctive approach to conflict and to criticism? Do you fight back? Close down? Take on the mantle of guilt?
- Would the people in your life agree with your analysis? Can they predict your reactions to conflict and criticism?

TECHNIQUE #7:
Understand Your Power Base

Another part of knowing yourself is understanding where your power lies. Most people never stop to analyze their unique strengths and advantages, so they never use them as effectively and consciously as they might.

These questions will help you pinpoint your power base:

- What *natural advantages* do you enjoy in life: intelligence, good looks, sense of humor, charm, kindness, drive, patience, sensitivity, the ability to see the big picture, the ability to focus exclusively on one task? There are hundreds of characteristics that can give you a natural advantage. List thirty of your specific natural advantages.
- What are the *top skills* that you've developed over the years, or that you come by naturally?
- Which *people* in your life are part of your power base, and which new people could be included? These are people who support you either in tangible ways or by aligning mentally with your success.

    - Who are your key allies at work and at home?
    - Who are some potential allies? These people may be found in unlikely places.
    - What can you do to bring these potential allies into your circle of support?

Many of the questions in this chapter will take some thought, and some will be uncomfortable to answer. All of them will help clarify who you are and what is important to you. You deserve the time it takes to answer them.

The better you know yourself, the more authentically and powerfully you can answer Step One—"What do I want?"—and build the foundation for getting it.

EXERCISES

Schedule time out to think about and write down answers to the questions in this chapter.

STEP TWO:
Find Out What They Want and Make Them Feel Heard

CHECK YOUR ASSUMPTIONS

Problems seldom exist on the level at which they
are expressed.

—Zen saying

Step Two—Find out what they want and make them feel
heard—is a gold mine of negotiating benefits. Asking people
what they want does several important things:

1. It captures people's attention and creates a positive bond
   between you. They think you are a smarter, better person because you are interested in them and what they
   want.
2. Asking what they want forces you to speak first to their
   needs, which makes them listen better, sooner, and
   longer when it is your turn to talk.
3. You get the information you need to put together your
   proposal and present it effectively.
4. When they know you've heard what they said, they are
   far more likely to listen to you.

Forgetting or ignoring Step Two can be disastrous. When
people don't feel heard, they tend to tune out, get defensive,
give in to their own anger, and escalate the conflict.

When they *do* feel heard, the results can be equally dramatic. Even the worst situations can turn around quickly and
completely.

Dwight worked in Memorial Hospital's billing office. He knew that his two o'clock meeting with Kay Odell would be a challenge. Her husband had had bypass surgery and the insurance hadn't covered as much as she'd thought it would. She had already screamed at him over the phone, and she looked no calmer when she marched into his office, slapped a pile of bills on his desk, flung herself into a chair, and launched into a tirade.

She yelled about how unfair the whole health system was, how many of the tests and procedures had been unnecessary and wasteful, how the costs were inflated, how it wasn't fair to treat sick people this way, and how she was going to sue the hospital for every cent it was worth.

Dwight threw his hands up as if to defend himself and said, "Wait! Mrs. Odell, let's talk about this. I'm sure we can work something out." Kay hesitated just long enough for Dwight to start Step Two.

"I understand that you're upset and I'm sure you have good reasons, but let's see if we can't figure out what to do together. Why don't you tell me exactly what you want? I'm not saying I can give you all of it, but we have to start somewhere. How do you think we could resolve this fairly?"

Kay didn't have a lot of experience in being asked what she wanted, and she started by saying she only wanted to pay half of what the hospital had billed. Dwight wrote that down, and asked, "What else?"

"I'll need at least two years to pay it," she said. Dwight wrote that down, and asked her what else she wanted. Eventually, Kay had a chance to say all the nasty things she'd been wanting to say about the hospital and to make all her demands, both reasonable and unreasonable.

This was a great deal more than she had expected from the meeting; she felt heard and respected for the first time in her long and difficult association with Memorial. She'd thought that some bureaucrat would scream at her, "Pay the money today or we'll have you thrown in jail." Instead, Dwight seemed genuinely interested in her case, in learning about her grievances and needs, and in coming up with solutions. Already, she felt better and started to calm down.

After about twenty minutes, Kay had said everything she wanted to say and had told Dwight all the things she wanted.

He looked across the table and saw a reasonable, clear, and confident woman—someone with whom he could negotiate.

They started talking and were able to work out a compromise. The hospital's auxiliary maintained an emergency fund for patients like Kay's husband, and it could absorb a quarter of the costs. Kay would have to pay the other three-quarters, but the hospital had no problem with working out a payment schedule that she could handle. There were no more threats of lawsuits, and everyone involved was pleased with the agreement.

Dwight not only calmed Kay down by making her feel heard and respected, but he also gained the information he needed to put together a proposal and reach an agreement. If he hadn't been willing to invest twenty minutes in doing that, the hospital might have been saddled with a nuisance suit and Kay could have created a great deal of antagonism in the community.

If finding out what people want and making them feel heard is so powerful, why don't more people do it? One reason is that they haven't done Step One and aren't sure what they themselves want. It's hard to listen to others when you haven't figured out your own agenda and satisfied your own needs.

Another reason people don't listen to others is that they've already figured out the whole situation based on their own conscious or unconscious assumptions. They've decided what's going on, who is right, and what should be done—and they aren't interested in hearing anything that might contradict their opinion. The people across the table from them don't feel heard because they *haven't* been heard.

TECHNIQUE #8:
Recognize Your "Hot Buttons" and the Assumptions Through Which You See the World

We see things as *we* are, not as *they* are. We see what we *expect* to see, not necessarily what is actually there.

Beliefs shape our experience, not the other way around.

Often, these beliefs take the form of hidden assumptions that we don't even know we have. Assumptions that stay hidden can sabotage any negotiation. It's almost impossible to hear what people say when you've already decided who they are and what they want.

To do Step Two successfully, you have to be alert to these hidden assumptions, bring them up to the conscious level, and recognize them for what they are—assumptions, not necessarily the truth. Step Two requires hard facts and accurate information; you can't speak to their needs or make good proposals if you're proceeding on the basis of speculation, fears, hopes, biases, or hidden beliefs.

We often forget how much we assume. A teacher in Marin County, California, asked her second-graders the meaning of the word "pause." A little girl raised her hand and answered with great certainty, "That's when you're watching your VCR and you have to go to the bathroom so you push that button."

Later that same day, the teacher took a child to the office to call his mother. He stared blankly at the rotary dial on the phone and asked, "How do you use *that?*"

You can't get on the same wavelength with someone when you're only tuned to one channel—yours. Step Two means moving around on the dial and tuning into other people's frequencies.

You don't have to change your biases and beliefs; you just have to know what they are so that you can make allowances for them and not treat them as reality.

Hot Buttons

One way to check your biases is to make a list of likes and dislikes. Write down your top three likes and dislikes in these categories: concepts, people, and what you like or dislike about them. My client Tim's list looked like this:

Concepts I Like	*Concepts I Dislike*
1. Responsibility	1. Betrayal
2. Freedom	2. Cheating
3. Sense of humor	3. Laziness

People I Like and What I Like About Them
1. Wife—Responsible/Gentle
2. Son—Humorous/Intelligent
3. Secretary—Loyal/Humorous

People I Dislike and What I Dislike About Them
1. Former partner—Cheating
2. Employee—Lazy/Wants a free ride
3. Neighbor—Lies

Your dislikes are probably your hot buttons, the areas around which you are most likely to get upset and react emotionally. Cheating and laziness are particular hot buttons for Tim. He is probably more likely to get upset about those issues than about others that don't appear on his lists.

The first step in managing your hot buttons or in eliminating unwanted assumptions is to recognize what they are. As you start becoming aware of them and noticing the effect they have on your work and on your peace of mind, you can begin to let them go.

Knowing what your hot buttons are also lets you plan ahead. When you know you'll encounter someone who is likely to press them, apply the Look Ahead Rule.

The Look Ahead Rule: Take time before you see the person to look ahead and imagine what you will do the next time he or she exhibits the behavior that bothers you.

- What will you do?
- Then what will the other person do?
- Then what will you do?

This lets you "script" the encounter and think through your reactions ahead of time so that you're prepared for those hot buttons to be pressed and can choose your reactions.

Your dislikes may also be qualities you dislike about yourself or issues that are unresolved from childhood. Tim's father may have cheated on his mother, or punished Tim severely for cheating—or perhaps Tim is cheating in some area of his life. His particular difficulty with laziness may also come from unresolved childhood issues, or he may unconsciously fear that he himself is lazy. *Unresolved issues often involve things we got too little of, or too much of, when we were children.*

Your "likes" may represent the qualities you most like in yourself, the core of your highest and best self. Tim's fondness for humor and being responsible may reflect characteristics he particularly likes about himself.

It may be uncomfortable to examine these likes and dislikes, triggers, and hot buttons, but it will help you resolve the issues and keep them from getting in your way in the meantime.

Your Specific Assumptions

Pay particular attention to the assumptions you make about people because of their appearance, background, sex, position, attitude, or behaviors.

When Ben got off the plane from Los Angeles for his interview at a Chicago investment firm, the two partners meeting his plane knew they'd pegged him exactly right. From his haircut down through his expensive sunglasses and sportcoat to his fancy loafers, everything about Ben's appearance screamed, "I'm from L.A. and I'm cool."

The partners, Ken and Frank, thought they knew what people from L.A. were like: laid-back, shallow, concerned with external appearances and having a good time, into cheap thrills and possibly drugs. They stifled smiles, thinking of the weekend through which they would be "forced" to escort Ben after the Friday-morning interview.

Despite learning that Ben had two children and was interested in finding a place to settle permanently, they took him on a tour of the hottest places in town, kept the liquor flowing and the drugs available, and offered to make sure he didn't spend the nights alone.

Ben had been impressed with the firm from a professional viewpoint and was polite all weekend, but left with the impression that Chicago wasn't the kind of place he wanted to raise his children and that it didn't lend itself to the stable, church-centered life that he and his wife enjoyed.

The assumptions that Ken and Frank made based on Ben's appearance cost them a valuable colleague.

Our society is in transition. Assumptions that might have

been generally accepted fifty years ago—that women prefer to work in the home, for instance, or that men with long, unkempt hair are sloppy, untrustworthy, and possibly incompetent—may no longer have any basis in reality. Most women now prefer to work outside the home. Many men with long, messy hair are the high-tech geniuses of our age, and billionaires as well.

Today, no assumption based on appearance, background, sex, position, attitude, or behavior is universally true, and the old beliefs can get you into terrible trouble very quickly.

The first key to avoiding these unconscious assumptions is to identify them. You are probably aware of many of these beliefs and biases, but may be unaware of others. These questions will help pinpoint some hidden assumptions.

Appearance

What can people's appearance tell you about them?

What does it mean when they look neat or sloppy, clean-cut or punked out, cheaply or expensively dressed?

Do light and dark hair say different things to you? Short and tall? Slim and heavy?

What other assumptions do you make about people based on appearance?

Background

What assumptions do you make based on race? What are your general beliefs about white people, black people, people of Asian descent, Europeans, American Indians? How would you react to learning that you would be working with someone from each of these groups? Working *for* them?

What stereotypes do you have about people of various European descents: Irish, Italian, Greek, British, Scandinavian, French, German?

Can you tell when someone is from a wealthy or a poor background? How? What difference does it make in that person?

What other beliefs do you have based on background or ethnicity?

Sex

If you are a man, do you resent the growing presence of women in the workplace and their increasing ability to rise through the ranks? Do you believe that women are less aggressive, less willing to go the extra mile in business? Are they *too* aggressive? How would you feel about having a woman for a boss? How would it be different from having a man for a boss?

If you are a woman, do you feel discriminated against and approach people at work with a chip on your shoulder and something to prove? Do you resent having to balance work and taking care of the home and children? How do you feel about other women in the workplace? Do you feel you are at an advantage working with or for a man, or a woman? Why?

What stereotypes do you have based on someone's sexual preference?

What other assumptions do you have about men or about women or their sexual preferences that may jeopardize your ability to see each individual as unique?

Position

Do you make assumptions about someone because he or she is your boss? What characteristics are bosses likely to have? How must you be when you are around bosses?

If you are the boss, what characteristics must you exhibit and how must you interact with those who work for you?

What are CEO's like? Secretaries? Middle-management people? Custodial staff?

Attitude

Do you assume that the new kid will be uncooperative because she's wearing a black leather skirt, spiked hair, and purple lipstick? She may be the computer whiz who makes your life a lot easier and brings cookies to work every Friday.

Because Stan never initiates a conversation, do you consider him unfriendly? He may be painfully shy.

Do you pile work on chirpy Suzie because she's so effervescent, such a good egg? She may be saying scathing things about you to half the people in the company.

Behaviors

Do you assume that people who smoke are dirty and undisciplined?

That people who take two-hour lunches are lazy freeloaders, possibly alcoholics?

That secretaries who file their nails at their desks are incompetent airheads?

That people who wear expensive clothing are inherently powerful? Or that they are shallow and concerned only with external appearances?

What other behaviors "tell you what a person is like"?

These assumptions aren't necessarily bad, and there isn't a person alive who doesn't make some of them. They just aren't very good barometers if you really want to know and honor the truth about another person, or if you want accurate information on which to base action or negotiation.

TECHNIQUE #9:
Find Out What They Want or Mean, Not What You Would Want or Mean If You Used the Same Words

Two people may do exactly the same thing, but intend two entirely different meanings. They may speak the same words, but mean to communicate two completely different messages.

Alex was new to the company and showed up fifteen minutes late for his meeting with Joan, who was also a middle manager at about the same level in the organization. She interpreted his lateness as an affront, a power play, a way of saying he didn't think she was all that important.

In fact, "fifteen minutes fashionably late" had been common practice at Alex's old company. There, a nine o'clock meeting had meant nine-fifteen, a four o'clock meeting had meant four-fifteen. This was an assumption that everyone had adopted over the years. To arrive for a nine o'clock meeting at nine o'clock was interpreted as overeager, an attempt to show up the other person.

Alex hadn't bothered to check this assumption, so he fell prey to Joan's very different assumption—that nine o'clock meant nine o'clock.

Find out what *they* mean by what they say and do, and don't assume it's the same as what *you* would mean.

When you manage people, remember that—

1. Everyone has his or her own individual set of assumptions about what certain words and actions mean.
2. Most people are unaware of what these unconscious assumptions are.
3. To communicate effectively, you have to discover what other people mean by what they do or say, and speak their language.

If you say the same words—"Thanks, that's fine"—to two employees when they hand you finished work, you may get two very different reactions. To one person, it may be high praise, a major acknowledgment. It may give him or her a tremendous sense of accomplishment and make his or her day. To another person, it may sound like a disparaging brush-off, damning with faint praise.

If you found yourself in this position, you would begin with Step One: Know exactly what you want. Your answer would probably be, "I want this person to feel acknowledged and to understand that I appreciate the quality of the work."

Then you would move on to Step Two, "Find out what they want and make them feel heard." If you didn't think the acknowledgment was getting through, you might say, "I'm very pleased with what you're doing, but I'm not sure the message is getting through. Is there something I can say or do to make sure you know how much I appreciate what you've done? I want you to have this 'win.' "

You might also want to find out more about the person, so that you can speak his or her language next time.

TECHNIQUE #10:
Don't Deduce Other People's Intentions from Your Fears

Most people share three main fears about solving problems and negotiating agreements. They assume that:

1. Their worst fears are what the other person actually intends to do.
2. They have a less powerful position than the other person.
3. Everyone wants the same thing from an agreement.

In fact, these fears are usually groundless. People rarely do the things you fear most. Your position is usually more powerful than you think. It is unusual for both people to want exactly the same thing from an agreement.

Any one of these fears can keep you from finding out what others want and making them feel heard. It's hard to listen or to acknowledge others when you're dreading the worst, feeling powerless, or making false assumptions about why they are there.

These fears are usually unconscious. They can muddy the waters even without your being aware of them. When you are aware you can make a conscious decision not to let them affect your negotiation.

Keep in mind that other people have these same unconscious fears, and that you can make things go more smoothly by putting their minds at rest.

TECHNIQUE #11:
Don't Assume You Know What People Want—
or That They Know What You Want—Just Because
You Know One Another Well

Get the facts, or the facts will get you. Don't assume that because you know people well or are close to them, you understand what they mean when they say something—and don't assume that they understand what *you* mean.

Todd had been designing the graphics that Mary used to advertise her needlework shop for five years. They had been friends since college, were very close, and saw one another socially with their spouses. Their children even went to the same school.

The work he did for her had always been very splashy and abstract. She loved it, and it had gotten good results. When it was time to design the fall ads, both of their schedules were very hectic. On the day they were supposed to meet, Mary's son broke his arm and she spent the afternoon at the hospital. She called Todd to say, "I don't see when we're going to be able to get together on this. Just go ahead, but make it all a little simpler this time."

"Fine," he said, assuming he knew just what she wanted.

In fact, she'd had something in mind that was quite different from what they'd been doing. She was thinking of just a few subtle lines, her logo, and the name of the shop. He was thinking "splashy and abstract, just *simpler* splashy and abstract."

The meeting at which the designs were unveiled was a disaster. They weren't at all what Mary wanted, and she was upset. Todd thought he had operated in good faith; they were "simpler."

It took a long time to sort through the problem, but both Todd and Mary learned a lesson. He learned to be especially clear and careful when dealing with friends, and she learned that she was as responsible for giving him good direction as he was for coming up with good designs.

TECHNIQUE #12:
When You Are With Someone You Like, Check Your Assumptions More Often, Because You Will Tend to Do It Less

Our most inaccurate communications are often with the people for whom we have strong feelings, the people we love or hate.

When we care for someone, we don't usually check our assumptions closely enough. We may think we know one another's shorthand and assume things that aren't necessarily true—or we may deliberately avoid questioning the other person because we don't want to disturb the relationship or have an unpleasant conversation.

Zack and Helen, husband and wife, had owned the family upholstery business for twenty years when he decided to get a new accountant and turn over much of the day-to-day bookkeeping to this man. Helen had a funny feeling in the pit of her stomach about this new arrangement, and a fleeting thought that she was a partner in the business and ought to check out the new accountant and the new procedures, but Zack seemed insulted when she asked to come to their meetings. She backed off to keep the peace. After all, he was her husband and she trusted him. He had always done a good job with the money, so she assumed that her fears were silly.

The new accountant wound up getting them into deep financial trouble, and Helen realized that she hadn't been careful enough.

This dynamic can also work in the opposite way. When dealing with people we *don't* like, we tend to be doubly careful and *over*check. All this second-guessing can make us appear defensive and distrustful, which can make them even more wary. This, in turn, sends us negative messages. Everyone's assumptions start to ricochet off one another, the communication gets impossibly muddled, and everyone comes away with mistaken impressions.

Nancy was an interior decorator and had scheduled a meeting with Tammie, a prospective client. That morning, Nancy was talking with another decorator when Tammie's name came up. The other decorator gasped and told Nancy that under no circumstances should she work for Tammie. She said that Tammie was extremely difficult, constantly changed her mind about colors and fabrics, and would make Nancy's life a nightmare.

Nancy walked into the meeting with trepidation. She was ill at ease and defensive, mistrusted everything Tammie said, and spent the whole time thinking about clauses she could put into their contract so that Tammie could never change her mind. Tammie found her sullen and unpleasant to be around, and didn't hire her.

It doesn't really matter whether or not Tammie would have been a difficult client—Nancy never got the chance to find out. If she had written Tammie off completely because she assumed the other decorator's comments were accurate, she could have simply canceled the meeting and saved herself some time. If she thought she might want the job anyway, it would have been in her interest to put her assumptions aside and approach Tammie objectively, without those negative biases.

Pay special attention to Step Two when dealing with people for whom you have strong feelings—positive or negative—and treat them as you would treat anyone else.

Make your Step Two more effective each time by continually checking your assumptions about people and by being alert to the biases you may bring to a situation.

EXERCISES

1. What assumptions are you most likely to make about others?
2. How does this put you at a disadvantage in dealing with them?
3. What can you do to make sure you check your assumptions closely?

SEE THE WORLD
AS THEY DO

Negotiations are about whatever the parties
involved think they are about.

—HOWARD RAIFFA

In the last chapter, you examined assumptions that could
color your interactions with others. This chapter is about discovering what *other people's* assumptions, motivations, and values are so that you understand them better, get a clearer idea
of what they mean by what they say, and complete Step Two
more quickly and accurately.

To find out what people want, you have to see the world
as they do. That means putting yourself in their shoes and
understanding their point of view—even when you don't
agree or are engaged in a heated argument.

Much of this information about others can—and should—
be collected before you actually sit down to solve the problem
or work out the agreement. Stay alert to clues and continue
to gather information as you talk, but give yourself an advantage by finding out as much as possible before you meet.

TECHNIQUE #13:
See Their World Their Way

Being "right" or "good" may not be as important to the negotiation as knowing what *they* think is "right" or "good." Step outside yourself to see how other people perceive the situation, so that you can speak and act in ways that they understand. If you try to act "good" or "right" without making sure that they share your ideas about what these qualities mean, you may be surprised at others' reactions.

Sales skyrocketed the year that John Kenwood took Paul on as a junior partner in his hardware business. Paul brought new life and new ideas to Kenwood's well-established small-town store, and the older man wanted Paul to have a voice in determining what they did with the profits.

Paul had been raised to value thrift and saving. To him, the "right" answer to Kenwood's question was "Save it for a rainy day, or put it back into the business." Kenwood's values were different. His attitude was "You can't take it with you, and everyone should put something back into the commu-nity." His idea had been to fund the landscaping for a small park in the downtown area, or perhaps to open a community day-care center for working mothers.

Paul believed he was scoring points with his suggestions, but Kenwood thought his ideas lacked vision and were some-what selfish and money-grubbing.

Paul only looked at the situation from his own perspective. He never got behind Kenwood's eyes and saw his world his way. You have to do what you think is right, but don't assume that others will automatically agree it's the "right" or "good" thing to do.

Abby wanted to spend less time at the design firm she had founded six years earlier, and hired Laura to manage the business and the designers she employed. These people tended to be renegades who worked odd hours, were vocal about their disagreements, and could often be found watching soap operas in the afternoon, then slaving away at their draw-ing boards in the dead of night.

Laura decided she was going to bring some order to the

place. She instituted regular working hours, laid out mediation procedures to deal with disagreements, and banned television from the office. The employees went nuts, business fell off, and Abby had to come back to work.

Laura's changes would have been applauded in most businesses, but they didn't work in this particular situation. She hadn't bothered to look at Abby's business through Abby's eyes.

TECHNIQUE #14:
Learn to Identify Other People's Assumptions, Motivations, and Prejudices, and What They Consider Threats or Opportunities

Find out all you can about people's backgrounds, viewpoints, and passions so that you know—

- What excites them.
- What puts them to sleep.
- What frightens them.
- Who they are at work.
- Who they are when they leave the office.
- What they really want from life—and how they think they can get it.

You can learn a lot about people through the choices they make. Research decisions they've made in the past. If you head an accounting firm that wants a certain manufacturer's business, find out why they chose not to make that major expansion three years ago. Did the owner want it to remain a small, family-style business? Is he just timid and conservative? Did he know something that others didn't about the future of that market? Does he still feel as he did then?

Knowing the answers to these questions not only saves you from putting your foot in your mouth, it lets you design your presentation so that you and your ideas are aligned with his wants and needs.

If you can't do this research before you meet, extract the information as you talk. You may not want to push him up against a wall and demand aggressively, "Hey, why did you turn down that golden opportunity (you idiot)?" You can, however, establish a connection with him by talking about other things and then asking casually, "I've always been intrigued by that decision not to expand. Can you tell me about it?"

These questions can help you determine what makes people tick, so that you can better negotiate Step Two and speak to them in language they can understand.

Their Assumptions and Motivations

- How do they spend their time and money?
- Who are their heroes and heroines?
- Who and what excites them most? Why?
- Who and what most threatens them? Why?
- What are their career goals, and how do they plan to advance those goals? What kinds of things do they perceive as opportunities?
- What are the key elements in their belief system? Are there strong "rights" and "wrongs"? What qualities do they value most? What qualities do they dislike most?

Their Background

- What is their personal background? Age? Sex? Ethnicity? Place in the birth order? Health status?
- What is their personal environment like? This includes hometown, family structure, schooling, work friendships, interests, and life-style.
- What is their organizational culture and how does it affect them? What personality and work styles are rewarded in their organization? Who was their first boss? Their mentor?
- What changes have they made recently?
- What major issues are pending in their lives?

- Who are their important peers, allies, and leaders? What is important to these people?

Your Agreement

- What pressures or possible stumbling blocks might they see in your negotiation? Time? Money? Other issues?
- What are their alternatives to reaching an agreement with you?
- What may be their objections to your proposal?
- What can you do to work around those objections?

TECHNIQUE #15:
Remember That Most People Are Not Aware of Their Own Prejudices, Assumptions, and Hot Buttons

Most people go through life assuming that their viewpoint is the only true or right way to see the world. They don't bother to check their assumptions, and often aren't even aware that many of their ideas are just that—assumptions and prejudices. They assume that when their hot buttons are pushed, they are simply experiencing righteous indignation.

It's not your job to point out the error of their ways. You can't march up to people and deliver a lecture: "Hey, mister, do you realize you're the only person in this room who thinks we have a right to dump toxic waste into that river because what's good for business is good for America?"

Since you can't change people, or at least can't count on changing them, you have to work around these preconceptions if you want to forge an agreement.

Sam was the business consultant for a company that presented "success workshops." The owner, Martha, had an extravagant vision of her own success and grandiose ideas about becoming "a multimillion-dollar corporation" despite the fact that she was barely making ends meet.

Martha had demanded that her sales force double its figures

in the coming year, and decided that the company should move to larger, more elaborate, and more expensive offices based on these projections.

Sam's eyes nearly rolled back in his head when he heard this news. Morale in the beleaguered sales department was already understandably low, and it seemed unlikely that the sales force would meet the new quotas. Costly new offices would spell financial disaster.

Sam did have two advantages:

1. He knew where Martha's hot buttons were.
2. He knew that she did *not* know where they were.

Sam knew that if he made any reference to not having "made it" yet, or to possible failure, Martha would see red, fly into a rage, and fire him as she had fired two business consultants before him.

His challenge was to prevent the expensive move without telling Martha that she couldn't afford it. Instead of talking about minimum profits, unpaid bills, and dwindling enrollment in the success workshops, he spoke of the current "landlord's market," of the lack of appropriate office space, and of the possibility of putting money aside now so that Martha could buy her own building a few years down the road.

He knew that Martha wouldn't like the idea of getting bamboozled or being forced to rent inferior office space, and that the idea of owning her own "corporate headquarters" would appeal to her vision of herself and the company.

Sam worked around Martha's assumptions, prejudices, and hot buttons, rather than trying to enlighten her about them. If she'd been ready for that kind of information about herself and her limitations, she probably would have sought it elsewhere. If Sam had brought it to her attention, he would have been pouring gas on a fire.

By understanding her perspective and recognizing that she was not examining her own assumptions, he was able to save both the company and his own job.

To do Step Two effectively, you have to see the world as others see it. When you have the ability to walk a mile in their moccasins, you can find out what others want and make them feel heard much more quickly and completely.

EXERCISES

1. Recall a time when you were able to see the world as someone else saw it, and be more effective in the situation as a result.
2. Recall a time when you weren't able to do this. What happened in the negotiation? How did you feel about it?
3. Did someone ever fail to see the world through your eyes in a conflict or negotiation? How did it feel? How might you have reacted differently if you had felt understood?

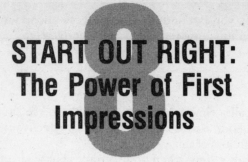

START OUT RIGHT:
The Power of First Impressions

If you begin with a loud voice, you soon leave yourself nowhere to go but to fists.
—Ikaku Masao, martial arts expert

Have you ever met someone and known immediately what that person was like? First impressions are the most powerful, and many first impressions are formed before a word is spoken. Nonverbal communication often speaks most loudly.

We make judgments about people within seven to twenty seconds, and research shows that these first impressions are extremely difficult to change. They can last a lifetime.

This chapter is about making first impressions that put others at ease and create immediate rapport so that you can move smoothly through Step Two: Find out what they want and make them feel heard.

TECHNIQUE #16:
Start Out Right: Make a Good First Impression

People are more likely to tell you what they want—

- If they like you.
- If they trust you.

- If they respect you.
- If they think you really want to know.
- If you've made it safe and easy for them to open up.

A good first impression creates these conditions.

By the same token, it may be very difficult to get the information you need if they don't like or trust you, or if you've created a negative first impression. Unfortunately, people's negative reactions are quicker and stronger and last longer than their positive ones. If we don't like or trust someone, we literally have trouble hearing that person.

Why do we instinctively like and respect some people, and dislike or distrust others? How do we make judgments about credibility, intelligence, and even honesty? How are first impressions formed?

Our first and most lasting impressions come from a primitive part of the brain; they are based on survival. Many subtle factors enter into this process, but as a general rule: *We like and trust people who are most like us.* The more different you are from another person in terms of age, sex, ethnicity, or position, the more barriers you may have to overcome and the more important it is for you to establish rapport early on.

Dawn was an Asian-American woman in her twenties. Her meeting that afternoon was with Elliot, a white man in his forties. She didn't want them relating to one another on the basis of stereotypes, and knew she had to find common interests that would create a bond. She did some research and discovered that they had both graduated from Stanford, lived in the same area, and had two children. Those were the bridges she used to make the connection quickly.

Your areas of commonality may be shared leisure or political interests, people whom you both know, personal histories, or common past activities. The bridge may be as simple as having the same productive approach to a business deal or job, or it may be nothing more than a common interest in the task that brings you together. That's all you need, if you put it to work for you and make the connection. Whatever the common ground, it's important to find it early on.

The issues of age, sex, ethnicity, and position are somewhat beyond your control, but the most important component in

creating a good first impression—nonverbal communication
—is not.

TECHNIQUE #17:
Use Nonverbal Communication to Establish Rapport

Actions speak more loudly than words. What you *don't* say often screams so loudly that people can't hear your verbal message. The way you move, gesture, sit, smile, and look at others can make the difference between success and failure.

Linguist Edward T. Hall says that 60 to 75 percent of the meaning of any conversation is buried in nonverbal language. Without saying a word, or even being aware of what you are doing, you can create the impression of being weak or powerful, credible or untrustworthy, aggressive or passive, likable or unlikable.

Even the best proposals, information, or suggestions may be disregarded if you aren't perceived as being powerful, credible, or trustworthy.

Knowing what your natural body language says, and learning to manage it so that it says what you want it to say, is a vital part of creating a good first impression.

Nonverbal communication takes place on several levels: movement, tone of voice, body position, eye level, smiling, and touching.

Here are a few guidelines.

Body Movement: Less Is More

Researchers agree that movement is the most influential part of nonverbal communication. The fewer hand and body gestures you make, the more powerful, deliberate, credible, and intelligent you appear to be.

Women have to be especially careful. One videotaped study of the ways in which women and men entered a room for a meeting showed that women performed an average of twenty-seven major movements. A woman might take off her coat, set down a briefcase, adjust her hair and skirt, pull items from her purse, and so on. The men performed only twelve such movements. People watching these tapes thought that women "took longer to become composed," and that this detracted from what they were there to say.

The women also had a tendency to "hand dance" during conversation—to make numerous gestures and movements from the elbows to the fingertips in order to make or emphasize points. When questioned, they said they were just releasing excess energy, but observers had the impression that they were "leaking" emotion. This, too, detracted from their overall impact.

Studies have shown that people who are perceived as leaders tend to *move less* and *gesture less*. The result is that their movements and gestures carry more weight and have more significance. People watch them and often unconsciously mirror their shifts in body position.

Suggestions:
- Avoid power-robbing "hand dancing," unnecessary gestures, and fidgeting.
- Make every movement count.
- Slow down your movements. When your movements are deliberate, considered, and thoughtful, that is how people will perceive you as well. As stripper Gypsy Rose Lee used to say, "Anything worth doing well is worth doing slowly."

Tone of Voice: Go Low, and Go Slow

The "nonverbal" part of voice concerns not what you say, but the tone and speed of your speech.

Again, less is more. People who speak in a lower tone, and those who speak slowly, are perceived as being more powerful and credible.

Suggestion:
- Be conscious of the speed and tone of your speech. Keep the pitch low; speak slowly and distinctly.

Body Position: Find Your Best Natural Poses

Leaders and people who are perceived as powerful take up more space than others do. They tend to lean slightly forward, with their arms and legs relaxed and slightly spread. By taking up more space, they appear to be taking charge.

This guideline works differently for men and women, and not just because women often wear skirts. Both men and women perceive that a woman's natural "space" is smaller than a man's.

I once watched a woman department head defeat her own purpose by trying to take up too much space. Just before she made an important point, she leaned back in her chair and put her arms across the empty chairs to either side of her. Every man in the room tensed up. One man told me later, "She thinks she's going to take over."

That was not what she intended to communicate, and it was certainly not what she said, but her body language had created that impression. The men resented her for it, even though they weren't aware of the reasons.

If she had put one arm—not both—across an empty chair, she would have appeared to be as powerful as the men but would have avoided "overstepping her bounds."

The more common situation is that women do not take up *enough* space. They tend to pull themselves in, hold their arms and legs close to their bodies, and either fidget or sit rigid and motionless—all of which tend to make them appear intimidated or victimized. By contrast, people perceived as powerful shift their position occasionally, which makes them appear relaxed, confident, and in charge.

These kinds of reactions and prejudices may not be fair or right—but research shows us that this is the way things are. People have these instinctive responses, whether we like it or not, and we have to take them into consideration in order to operate effectively.

The good news for women is that, although they tend to move more and take up less space, and therefore to be perceived as less powerful, they are much more alert to body language than men are.

Harvard psychologists developed a series of tests in which

men and women watched silent film clips of people talking and were asked to guess what was happening by "reading" their body language and expressions. Women accurately described the situation 87 percent of the time. Only men involved in "artistic" or "nurturing" occupations, such as nursing or teaching, performed as well.

Studies also show that asymmetrical body poses—in which the left side of your body is positioned differently from the right side—are more powerful than symmetrical ones. When you adopt a natural but slightly asymmetrical stance, you project a subtle confidence in yourself.

Suggestions:

- Train your body's "memory." Your body "remembers" and returns instinctively to certain positions, just as a garden hose returns to the position in which it has been lying. For each of the universal emotions (happiness, surprise, fear, sadness, anger, and disgust) you tend to adopt a pose that is uniquely yours. Ask a friend to observe you over the next few weeks and show you what you look like when you adopt those poses, and also what you look like when you seem most powerful and self-confident. Another way to get this information is to have someone videotape you in several role-playing situations.

  Find out what your instinctive poses are, and determine whether they work for you. Do you want to keep them, or to practice new ones?

  When you know your naturally happy, confident, and powerful poses, you can adopt them even when you are feeling unhappy or weak. This keeps you from being at a disadvantage in a negotiation, and may actually make you feel better. Your body's natural feedback process helps you feel more positive and powerful when you are in these positions.

- Adopt a slightly asymmetrical pose. Turn slightly to one side. Rest your chin on one hand, not two. Lean forward with one arm on the table. These poses make you appear more powerful and self-assured.

Eye Level: Give Them an Eyeful

Studies show that in a group, the person whose eye level is highest is usually perceived as the leader. People turn to address that person first.

Sarah was a five-foot, two-inch attorney. She was frustrated because although she'd been on an intergovernmental council for three years, she couldn't speak two sentences without being interrupted. Finally she took a new tack. At one particularly important meeting, she walked to the side table and slowly poured herself a cup of coffee just before she wanted to speak. When she turned, still standing, to address the group, her eye level was the highest in the room. She had their complete attention.

The others perceived her as a leader because they literally had to look up to her. *How* she conveyed her information mattered as much as what she actually said.

Suggestion:
- Stand tall, and sit high. When you want to make sure people are listening, adjust your position so that your eye level is higher than theirs.

Smiling: Smile for All the Right Reasons

Smiling is a double-edged sword, especially for women, who tend to smile more than men do. Smiling can make you seem friendly, attractive, and open—but it can also be seen as a gesture of appeasement or as a sexual invitation, especially when combined with body postures that suggest either of these attitudes.

Social psychologist Nancy Henley calls the smile "a woman's badge of appeasement" and demonstrates that women often use it to placate men. According to her research, the more a woman smiles, the more she is perceived as a victim—and women smile 89 percent of the time in social encounters, as opposed to only 67 percent for men.

Suggestion:

- Smile to establish connections, convey friendliness, and when it is appropriate—but don't "oversmile" or use smiling as a gesture of appeasement. Remember that, especially when women combine smiling with suggestive posture, it can be interpreted as a sexual invitation.

Touching: Touch to Establish Intimacy, Not Destroy It

People are comfortable with various levels of physical intimacy, and you have to judge where they—and you—are on that spectrum. Touching can create connections or destroy them.

Generally, the safest and least threatening way to touch someone is to shake hands. You introduce a bit more intimacy when you shake hands by putting your left hand on top of the other person's. Even more intimate is shaking hands and placing your left hand on the other person's upper arm.

Suggestion:

- Be sensitive to other people's comfort levels with touching, and react appropriately.

Learn to Self-Correct

There are no pat answers in nonverbal communication. You have to stay alert to others' reactions, recognize when what you're doing isn't working, and learn to self-correct.

Andrea owned a printing business. She had met Jane socially and learned that she was a graphic designer looking for a printer whom she could use regularly. They decided to meet for lunch the next week.

When they sat down in the restaurant, Andrea wanted Jane to know how competent and successful she was, and did a number of things to suggest power. She leaned forward with both arms on the table, sat up straight so that her eye level was higher than Jane's, minimized her gestures, and spoke slowly in a low tone.

She could see that she was succeeding—Jane was definitely

getting the picture that Andrea was a powerful person—but she could also see that it wasn't working. Jane wasn't looking for someone powerful and dominating; she was more interested in cooperation and teamwork. After all, she was the designer and she was going to be calling the shots if they worked together. Jane didn't want a printer who was weak, but she did want one who would do as he or she was told.

Fortunately, Andrea saw what was happening and could change her nonverbal communication to correct the impression of an arrogant, defiantly independent and powerful printer.

She leaned back in her chair, smiled, and folded her hands in her lap. She stopped talking about her ideas and started to question Jane about her needs and wants. When she was sure what Jane wanted, and that Jane understood she wasn't trying to steamroll her, she added a few ideas of her own. Their collaboration turned out to be a pleasant, profitable one.

When you understand what your nonverbal communication is saying, you are ahead of the game. With practice, you can make it say what you *want* it to say.

TECHNIQUE #18:
Play with Your Full Deck

People are more open to you when you reflect the part of yourself that is most like them. Playing with your full deck means using all your skills, talents, abilities, and knowledge to get in sync with others and establish an immediate connection. It means bringing forward the parts of yourself that are most like them so that they feel comfortable opening up and talking about what they want.

People who survive and thrive are those who can select a response from a broad range of possible behaviors. In nature, this is called "requisite variety." The chameleon is a good example. He remains true to himself—he is still a chameleon, regardless of what color he chooses to be—but he survives and prospers because he can bring various aspects of himself to the surface to match his surroundings.

Psychologist Abraham Maslow said, "If all you have is a hammer, you treat everything as a nail." You have much more than a hammer—Triangle Talk gives you a whole chest full of tools—and it doesn't work to treat everybody the same way. Each person is a unique individual and deserves your full attention.

Step Two depends on finding out as much as you can about what others want; use everything at your disposal to connect with them quickly and get that information. Here are some cards that you may want to play from your deck.

Mirroring

One way to reflect the part of you that is most like others is to mirror their body posture, movement, and tone or rate of speech.

Ron could see when he sat down to help Tim refinance his mortgage that Tim was either naturally shy or nearly catatonic at the prospect of looking at all these figures and paying closing costs. Tim sat slumped in his chair, his arms crossed and his eyes darting around the room.

Ron was a naturally outgoing, high-affect, jovial person. He tended to speak loudly and quickly, to pump people's hands, and to have a great time cutting deals—but he was also aware that these tendencies didn't work in every situation, and knew how to play with his full deck. Because his own habits were so flamboyant and could easily work to his disadvantage, Ron had had many opportunities to practice mirroring.

In the meeting with Tim, he had to keep reminding himself: "Gently, softly, slowly." He could tell as soon as he walked in the door that Tim wasn't going to break any bones shaking his hand, and softened his own grip to match Tim's.

When they sat down, Ron didn't lean forward onto Tim's desk, but sat back in his chair as Tim was doing—making sure that their eyes were on about the same level. He knew that Tim wouldn't respond well to being pressured, and gave a low-key presentation of the refinancing, making sure that Tim understood everything he was saying even if he had to go very slowly.

As the meeting progressed, Tim became more comfortable and more assertive. He asked more questions and even made some jokes. Ron kept pace with him, but never outdid him, and the refinancing was a success for both men.

Mirroring can sometimes put you on the same wavelength in a way that no words could, but it must be done subtly. You don't want to look as if you're mocking the other person or using positions that are unnatural for you. Be sensitive to what others are thinking and feeling, and do what makes them most comfortable.

Self-Inflicted Humor

Telling one on yourself almost always creates rapport. It's hard not to like someone who can laugh at himself or herself. This technique is particularly helpful if you seem to have greater authority than the other person and want to even out the balance of power.

William was a small, rather quiet man who'd had such success managing the accounting department that he was promoted to head of sales. He was a coach-style boss who asked a lot of questions and listened to his staff.

The aggressive sales department was experiencing a great deal of internal turmoil, and William was both excited and daunted at the prospect of leading these mavericks with his slow, careful, considered style and his lack of sales experience.

He opened the first meeting by saying, "I'm honored to be here. I know many of you are wondering why a high-powered person like myself was placed in charge of such a mild-mannered crew."

Self-inflicted humor was the perfect card to play in this situation. Rather than ignoring what was on everybody's mind, he spoke to the issue directly and aligned himself with their concerns.

He went on to strengthen the connection with a poignant personal story that also told one on himself. He wanted the people in sales to know that he was committed to them and determined to support their success over the long term.

"I met my wife at a cocktail party thirty years ago," he began. "I saw her across the crowded room and fell in love on the spot. Transfixed, I picked up a small crystal bowl of olives, walked over to her, and said, 'Here is a bowl of olives. I wish they were pearls.' It wasn't love at first sight for her, but I knew I could make her happy. A year later, she agreed to marry me and she has been the light of my life.

"After our thirtieth-anniversary party, the children came back to our house and she sat down in her favorite chair. I picked up a small crystal bowl I'd hidden earlier and held it out to her, saying, 'Here is a bowl of pearls. I wish they were olives. I've enjoyed every day with you and I intend to keep making you happy.'

"That, I think, is what life is about. Finding what we're willing to commit to and sticking with it. Proving we mean it—to ourselves and the ones closest to us. It may not be love at first sight between us, either, but I intend to be persistent in my support. Check where I've been. Watch what I do. I'm determined to give you everything you need to have all the satisfaction and success you can in your job. Thank you."

He sat down to thunderous applause.

The Memory Is in the Motion

Something special happens when two people move together—whether they are biking, playing racquetball, or simply walking down a corridor. A connection is established. They remember more clearly what is said, and both are apt to react more favorably to what is discussed. The movement itself seems to build trust and support.

Leanne had been Dennis's legal secretary for five years and believed she deserved a substantial raise. He thought she was asking for too much and would only agree to half the increase she requested.

Their disagreement was unusual—they were used to being on the same team—and made both of them feel somewhat betrayed. They had admired and respected one another. Now he thought she was only in it for the money, and she thought he didn't appreciate her.

The discussion got more heated and tempers began to flare when Leanne suggested they stop talking about the raise for a half hour and go for a walk. Even walking around the busy downtown streets seemed to relax both of them and put things into perspective. When they returned to the office, they were connected again and able to agree on a compromise—three quarters of what Leanne had originally requested.

The connection that comes from movement and physical activity works in degrees. From "most effective" to "least effective," they are:

- Both of you are involved in the activity.
- You are moving but the other person is not.
- The other person is moving but you are not.
- Both of you are watching other people move.

If you want what you say to be remembered, create some conscious physical movement around you.

Practice Acting, Not Reacting, When Your Hot Buttons Are Pressed

Being aware of your hot buttons is more important when you first meet someone than at any other time. That's when that person can catch you by surprise, and also when he or she can do the most damage. Learn to act, not react, when you feel that panel lighting up.

Bob was a three-piece-suit type, fifty years old, who had worked his way up in the company. He knew he would have a hard time walking into the meeting with Glen, the new twenty-five-year-old computer whiz with lightning bolts cut into the sides of his hair and bony knees sticking through his torn jeans. Glen was making nearly twice Bob's salary.

Bob's department was being computerized, however, and he needed Glen's help. The two of them would be working together closely for several months, and Bob didn't want the relationship to get off on the wrong foot. He knew that it was in his own best interest to manage his reactions and not let his hot buttons get the better of him.

Bob devoted some time each day in the week before their initial meeting to working through those hot buttons and mentally rehearsing how he wanted the meeting to go, so that he could step back, play with his full deck, and choose his responses rather than getting caught up in knee-jerk emotional reactions.

TECHNIQUE #19:
Expect the Best of Yourself and Others

If you believe the world is going to treat you well, and act accordingly, it will. People will be drawn to your positive outlook and become more positive themselves in your presence.

Comedian Rick Reynolds tells the story of going to pick up a friend at the airport and watching everyone come off the plane wearing tired, grumpy expressions. Then an older couple came through the door and a little girl ran to them and embraced her grandparents. Rick found himself smiling at this heartwarming scene. When he looked up again, everybody getting off the plane seemed to be smiling.

You often get back exactly what you expect to get back. Andy, who sold health insurance, was scheduled to talk to Roger about insurance for his small company of ten employees, but he didn't have much hope of success. He knew that Roger was also meeting with the representative of another health insurance company whose rates and benefits were slightly more competitive.

Andy's boss took him aside before the meeting and gave him a pep talk. He told Andy to go in there as if he knew he was going to get the sale. He said that you never knew what was going to happen, and that the meeting wasn't worth having unless he was going to give it his best shot. To do that, he had to adopt a positive point of view and expect the best.

What Andy didn't know was that since the two companies' rates and benefits were so close, Roger considered the service he would receive from his agent as important as the terms. When Andy showed up with a positive attitude, expecting that Roger would see the benefits of a contract with his company, Roger was impressed. Their meeting, and the good feeling it gave Roger, made the difference. He decided that doing business with Andy's company was worth the minimal sacrifice he made in the terms of the policy.

Even in the most difficult circumstances, try to find something about the person or the circumstances that you can like, or at least respect. Then focus on that. This attitude can change the way you live. It can keep you from constantly bumping up against barriers, and help you sail through any situation.

First impressions are the most important. As you start becoming aware of the impression you are making and learn to manage those first reactions, you will find that Step Two becomes easier.

EXERCISES

1. The next time you meet someone, be aware of the first impression you are making. Play back the encounter afterward, as if you were looking at it on videotape. What first impression would you have if you had just met you?
2. When was the last time you went into a meeting or encounter with a strong idea of what was going to happen? Was your expectation positive or negative? How did the meeting turn out?

PLAY DETECTIVE

Ego, not content, causes the most communication
standoffs. Contrary to what is commonly believed,
most disagreements are caused not by conflict
over what people need but how they actually talk
and act about those needs.
—CARMINE DE LA ROSA

After you've established a connection by making a good first
impression, you can get down to the business of finding out
what people really want from your interaction or negotiation,
or why they did what they did that upset you.

This chapter focuses on the nuts and bolts of assembling
that Step Two information—even when they themselves don't
know exactly what they want.

TECHNIQUE #20:
Cast a Wide Net with Your Initial Questions

Begin with broad, general questions so that you don't eliminate any possibilities or miss any opportunities. Fish for
information—and cast a wide net.

People are often more comfortable answering general questions. Once they start talking, it's easier for them to get more
specific. If you pin them down to minutiae right away, they
can become defensive and close down.

If you find yourself in a heated argument, for instance, you'll probably have better luck with a general "Are you upset with me?" than you will with a more specific "Are you still angry because I missed that meeting last Tuesday?"

If you get a "yes" to "Are you upset with me?" you have engaged the other person in Step Two. That person has started to define the problem, which is a way of telling you what he or she wants. You can then start narrowing your questions. You might proceed along the lines of "Can you tell me what it's about?" or "Is it about last Tuesday?"

When you invite people to give you their broad overview, you get more information about where their real interests lie and what they consider important. You can pin down the specifics later, when you see which direction they are heading in.

If you were in charge of building an addition to someone's house, for example, you might narrow options and eliminate possibilities if you began, "Now as I understand it, you want eight hundred square feet of family room with a bath, and the whole thing should cost under forty thousand dollars. Right?"

A better, more general opening that allows for more possibilities would be "Tell me what you have in mind for the addition."

If you're ever at a loss for questions, remember the old newspaper reporter's standards:

- Who?
- What?
- When?
- Why?
- Where?
- How?

Lauren knew nothing about Gerry when he came to her for investment counseling. To steer him toward the kinds of investments that would work for him, she had to find out a lot about him in a short time.

She started with broad, general questions like the following:

- "What would you like to have as a result of our sessions?"
- "What are your long-range financial goals?"
- "What do you want your life to look like in thirty years?"

Then she asked him more specific questions about each area of his life—career, family, leisure, retirement, etc. She kept asking questions until she got a full picture of his life as it was then, and as he wanted it to be in thirty years.

These are the kinds of things they discussed:

Family

Lauren's broad opening question: "What are your financial goals for your family?"

Gerry's general response: "I want to provide for my children."

Lauren's narrower follow-up questions: "How many children do you have? How old are they now? How much does it cost per year to support them? What does it mean to 'provide for' them? At what point do you want to stop providing food, shelter, and clothing for them? Do they know that? Do you want to send them to college? How much will that cost? When will it start? Do you want to make sure you leave them something? How much? What amount do you need to put aside each year to make that dream a reality?"

Career

Lauren's broad opening question: "What are your general career goals?"

Gerry's general response: "I want to retire at sixty."

Lauren's narrower follow-up questions: "How much do you make now? How much can you reasonably expect to make each year until you're sixty? How much will you need to live each year after sixty? What amount must you save or invest each year to ensure that you have that amount?"

The nature of Lauren's work dictated that she ask general questions first and then follow up with more specific queries, but the principle has value in any situation.

Pam was a dental hygienist. There were certain medical and dental questions she had asked each patient, but she also knew that most people didn't enjoy having their teeth cleaned and that she might be able to make it less traumatic if she knew something about their past experiences, fears, and preferences.

She cast a wide net with her initial questions, asking things like these:

- "Do you have your teeth cleaned often?"
- "How has it been for you in the past?"
- "Do you enjoy having your teeth cleaned?"

As she gathered information and got a sense of how each patient felt about having his or her teeth cleaned, Pam's questions became more specific.

Sometimes just having a chance to talk about their past experiences released some of her patients' fear. Some of them told her that they found it easier with a topical anesthetic, a flavored jelly rubbed on the gums. Others said that they always took a couple of aspirin before they had their teeth cleaned, a tip she passed on to other patients. At the very least, they felt more relaxed because she had indicated an interest in them as people, not just teeth and gums. That in itself reduced some of the pain.

Never be afraid to ask questions. Only *not* asking questions can make you look stupid.

TECHNIQUE #21:
"Columbo" Them

Peter Falk's TV character is no fool; he just plays dumb so that people will trust him and open up to him. This shuffling, stumbling, bumbling detective appears so nonthreatening that even crooks seem to want to help him out.

Much of what Detective Columbo does involves nonverbal communication. He mirrors people's body posture: if they slouch all over a couch, he slouches all over a chair. He adopts the same level of intensity: if they are laid-back, he takes it easy; if they scream, he screams.

Columbo is a master at drawing people out and getting them to talk about themselves by appearing interested and sometimes even naive. He never comes on too strong or tries to dominate the situation. Instead, he throws the ball back into their court and lets them come up with the answers.

He is so good at Step Two that all the rest of the techniques in this chapter are "Columbo techniques." Whenever you feel at a loss, ask yourself, "What would Columbo do in this situation?" You may not want to run out and get a crumpled raincoat, but otherwise he is an excellent model.

TECHNIQUE #22:
Avoid the "King of the Mountain" Approach

The King of the Mountain attitude says—verbally or, more often, nonverbally—that you're in charge, you have all the answers and all the power, you know what's best for everyone, and you're going to make sure the right thing happens. It implies that others are inferior, weak, stupid, passive, or easily manipulated.

Nobody likes to feel that way, and almost nothing puts people off as much as this caveman approach. What little control you may gain won't last long or be very satisfying. King of the Mountain power is based on domination and coercion, so it is easily eroded. This approach doesn't invite people to open up and tell you what they want.

You invite challenge and competition when you play King of the Mountain. Most people won't risk defying you, but a few will. Those who aren't cowering in the corner will be plotting to overthrow you. Don't forget how the game is played: as soon as one kid jumps up on a pile of dirt and yells, "I'm King of the Mountain," the rest swarm all over him to capture his throne.

TECHNIQUE #23:
Ask Open-Ended Questions

Open-ended questions can't be answered either "yes" or "no." They require some explanation and keep the other person talking.

Closed question: Do you agree with the proposal we were all sent in the mail?
Open-ended question: Before we talk about the proposal, tell me what you think we should do.

Closed question: Since we don't seem to be getting anywhere, do you want just to stop talking about this?
Open-ended question: We don't seem to be getting anywhere this way. What direction do you think we should take?

It's easier and safer for people to answer "yes" or "no" than to give a fuller explanation of what they want. They may jump at the chance to take themselves off the hook—especially if they are uncomfortable with conflict or potential conflict, or if they aren't clear about what they want.

Connie, the managing partner in her law firm, had just explained to ten of the attorneys her new system for keeping track of the hours they spent on each case. When she was finished presenting the new system, she noticed that Charles was sitting at the other end of the table with his arms and legs crossed, scowling down at a folder in front of him.

"Do you have a problem with this, Charles?" she asked. By asking a closed question that required only a "yes" or "no" answer, she forced him either to align with her when he clearly didn't want to do so (ensuring trouble down the road) or to polarize into a position against her, which is what he did.

"Yes, I think there are several things wrong with it," he said. Now it was Connie against Charles, and everyone at the table was consciously or unconsciously taking sides. This was not the result that Connie wanted, but she thought she was too far down the road to backtrack. She tried a power play that would force Charles either to toe the line or to appear guilty of insubordination.

"Well, can you live with it?" she asked. Another closed question. Another "yes" or "no" answer. In or out? Charles didn't want to put his job on the line because he couldn't adapt to a time-recording system, so he capitulated.

It looked like a victory for Connie, but it wasn't. No one at the table was impressed with the way she had handled the situation, and she now had a sleeping tiger in the office who resented what she'd done to him and was looking for a way to get back at her.

Connie could have avoided this conflict by asking open-ended questions. When she saw that Charles was unhappy, she could have given him an opportunity to voice his concerns without polarizing the situation and ending in a power play.

She might have said, "I'd like to hear your reactions to this, and see if you have any further suggestions. Charles?"

If she had listened to Charles's objections and honored his suggestions enough to consider them, they could have avoided a deeper conflict even if she didn't implement his ideas.

It's especially important to ask open-ended questions when others seem reluctant to speak up. If they are shy, upset, or afraid to say what they want, they are much more likely to retreat into "yes" and "no" answers, and you never find out what they really want.

Sally had fallen in love with the condominium that Patrick had showed her and had made an offer. The owners had made a counteroffer but insisted on taking the refrigerator with them. The negotiations went back and forth, getting increasingly unpleasant with each step. Sally developed the opinion that these people were monsters bent on punishing her, and that she couldn't possibly get a fair deal on that particular condominium. She became sullen and shut down, and even began to think that Patrick was working against her because he wanted the deal to go through at any cost.

Patrick was losing patience. He wanted the sale, but he didn't want to spend difficult weeks and months on what would actually be a relatively minor commission. He was tempted to pressure Sally into a "yes" or "no" decision and ask, "Are you in or out of this thing?" If he'd done that, she probably would have backed out.

Instead, he took her out to coffee and asked, "Sally, what

would it take for you to be happy with this deal?" That forced her to be creative and come up with solutions.

She thought a minute, then named a figure and added, "But I get the refrigerator and the dishwasher." He took the offer back to the other agent and said it was final. The deal was struck immediately.

Asking open-ended questions invites people to say more than they absolutely have to say and gives you more information about what they want.

TECHNIQUE #24:
Ask Advice

Columbo often asks advice—not because he doesn't know what to do, but to find out what others will say. It's a subtle way of getting people to tell you what they want. Sometimes they haven't even thought about it until you ask their advice on the issue. This technique makes them clear about what they want, and gives you the information at the same time.

Wes owned a stationery store and had always handled the very expensive, very fancy invitations for the annual benefit sponsored by Vicky's club. When the invitations arrived with the wrong date printed on them, they were both understandably upset. It turned out that Vicky had given him the correct date and he had made the error when the layout was delivered to the printer—but that Vicky had seen the proofs and approved them without noticing the mistake.

They both knew they were somewhat at fault, but not entirely to blame. The benefit was in two weeks, and something had to be done quickly. Both were angry and upset, but neither wanted to destroy the relationship.

Vicky thought of the triangle image, launched into Step One, and asked herself what she wanted. The best result would be for Wes to pay to have the invitations redone. Her bottom line, the minimum that she would accept, was that they split the cost of reprinting.

Next, she moved on to Step Two and asked Wes what he

wanted. He seemed either unsure or reluctant to tell her; he talked instead about how upsetting the situation was, how they could avoid it in the future, and how this had never happened to him before.

Finally, she said, "You know, Wes, I'm at a loss here. What do you think we should do? What's the best way to solve this situation quickly?"

When she asked advice and passed the problem back to him, he had no choice but to come up with an idea, or at least a place from which to start negotiating. He began tentatively, but gained confidence as he spoke. "Well, obviously I hate to incur the whole loss because you did approve those proofs, but I suppose there should be some way we could share the expense."

Now Vicky had at least some information. She knew that he felt partly responsible, but that he also thought she was partly responsible. She knew he hated to pay for something that wasn't entirely his fault, but also that he was willing to bend. She asked his advice again.

"What do you think is fair?"

"I'd be willing to pay for a third," he said.

This was less than Vicky's bottom line; half was the least that she was willing to accept. Instead of snapping this information back at him, she asked his advice again.

"You're in the business, Wes. Is there any other way to do this? Paying another two-thirds is just too much for us."

He thought for a minute, then came up with an idea that neither of them had considered. They could use the old invitations but enclose small, elegantly engraved cards noting the incorrect date and giving the correct one. The expense would be minimal compared to having the invitations reprinted. They would split the cost. It wasn't the ideal way to do things, but Vicky knew everyone would prefer that they save the money for their charity.

Asking advice not only establishes rapport and lets others know you respect them, but can also yield creative solutions.

TECHNIQUE #25:
Send Up Trial Balloons

Allow yourself to speculate about possible solutions and wonder aloud "What if . . . ?"

This technique works particularly well when—

- You are just starting to talk.
- Negotiations are stalled and you want to take a new direction.

Holly worked for an advertising agency that had just landed a new beverage account, and she was meeting with people from the soda company to talk about the approach they wanted to take. When she asked them directly, they didn't seem to want to talk. She figured that either they didn't have any specific ideas, or they were testing her and wanted to hear what she had to say.

She had worked out two or three approaches, but wanted to get some idea of where they were before she committed to one of them. She began by sending up some trial balloons:

"What I've found exciting about this campaign is that we have so many options, so many directions from which to choose. There are several approaches that could work . . ." Then she proceeded to speculate about how she might sell the soda to baby boomers or teenagers, from the point of view of health or delicious taste, and about various subtle messages that they could convey with each approach.

As she spoke, she watched their reactions and noted the ideas that elicited positive responses from them. She continued to float the other balloons, but kept coming back to those ideas. By the time she had finished her "Gee, there are so many ways to go . . ." speech, she had a good idea of what they would like and what they wouldn't.

TECHNIQUE #26:
Listen Actively

The best way to get a person to tell you more is to let that person know that you're listening. The best way to convey that information is to *be* listening. If you are listening actively—giving the person your full attention and responding to what that person says—he or she will know it.

Some of the classic ways to make sure the other person gets the message are:

- Nodding.
- Leaning forward slightly.
- Using the person's name.
- Paraphrasing the person's words.
- Verbal responses such as "Ah," "Ah-hah," "I see," and "I hear you."
- Requests for more information, such as "Tell me more about that."
- Recapping what the person has said, and then asking whether you have it right.

TECHNIQUE #27:
Start Out with Oblique Questions, Then Get Increasingly Specific and Direct

Start out indirectly, and work your way around to more direct questions.

Oblique, indirect questions:
- "What do you think of this situation?"
- "How is this affecting you?"
- "Have you heard any suggestions about how to solve this problem?"

More specific questions:
- "Exactly what would make this proposal work for you?"

- "What do you think we should do before we leave here today?"

Pete wasn't happy with Sherry's performance since she had returned to work after having her first child. She called in sick at least one day a week and was preoccupied when she did come to work. He suspected that she didn't have adequate child care and sympathized with her situation because he liked her and knew she could do good work, but he couldn't afford a half-time employee to whom he was paying a full-time salary.

When he did Step One, he saw that he only wanted to pay Sherry a full-time salary if she worked effectively full-time. He was willing for her to work part-time, but if she did that, she would have to take a cut in pay.

He suspected that Sherry was aware of the problem, but knew she wasn't eager to confront it. When they sat down to talk, he began with an oblique approach. He asked her about the baby and about how it was working for her to have a full-time job so soon after the baby's birth. He also asked about child care, and about any problems she might be having.

This gave him an idea of what her situation actually was and what her problems were. It also gave her a chance to get comfortable talking with him. Her mother was looking after the baby because Sherry couldn't afford full-time child care, but the mother's health was poor and she wasn't always up to caring for an infant. On days when her mother was ill, Sherry called in sick and stayed home with the baby.

After he had gathered all this information, Pete addressed the situation more directly to find out what Sherry wanted to do. "I have the feeling lately that we only have part of you here, Sherry," he began. "Your work is great when you're with us but you seem distracted and you've been taking a lot of sick days. I know you take a lot of pride in your work and I want this to work for you. I've thought about some alternatives and want to get your reaction."

Then he offered to let her work part-time or full-time. She said she needed to work full-time, so they started talking about other options for child care. At one point, Pete remembered another manager mentioning a woman in his department who was on maternity leave. Pete and Sherry thought she might want to earn some extra money and might enjoy taking care of Sherry's baby two or three days a week. Then Sherry's mother would only need to come over on the remaining two or three days. The plan worked well for everyone.

Asking oblique questions first is a way of easing people into telling you the truth—or helping them discover for themselves what it is.

TECHNIQUE #28:
Appeal to Their Positive Intent

Most people want a positive solution that works for everyone. No one wins if someone goes away angry or unhappy. We all act like children sometimes, but most of us can be brought back to reality when someone appeals to our positive intent.

Ruth managed a fast-food franchise that required its employees to have short haircuts or wear hairnets. Justin was a great worker, but someone had apparently forgotten to tell him about the hair regulations when he was hired. He absolutely refused to cut his shoulder-length blond hair or to wear a hairnet. He kept saying, "Hey, try to make me. I'll sue somebody."

Ruth didn't need the aggravation of the daily hairnet battle, she didn't want the franchise bothered with a nuisance suit, and she didn't want to lose Justin. This issue aside, he was pleasant, efficient, fun to have around, good for morale, and drew a large crowd of high-school girls after school each day.

She took him aside and said, "Look, Justin, I know you want your freedom of expression and all, but I want to put an end to this hairnet thing. It's making me nuts. I like you and you're a great worker. I want you here. I think, I hope, that you want to be here. There's nothing either of us can do about this rule. It's from national and we have to live with it. Let's just put it to bed so we can get back on the same team, have some fun, and make some money."

He burst out laughing, and showed up the next day with his long blond hair plastered to his scalp with a black hairnet. He looked a little strange, and Ruth suspected he meant to, but she had to smile. Neither of them ever mentioned the hairnet issue again.

Justin had meant well, and she had called on him to prove it.

TECHNIQUE #29:
Use Silence and Pauses

Any good reporter will tell you that if you want to find out what's going on, you don't fill up the silences in a conversation. Let the pause get a little longer, a little more awkward. People will start to feel uncomfortable and fill it up. If you still look puzzled or expectant, they will try to fill it up *more*. They will usually talk until they say what you want to hear.

Other people just need a little time to think when you ask them what they want. If you jump in to keep the conversation going, it distracts them and they can't come up with an answer because they're trying to listen to *you*.

Natalie was interviewing people for a receptionist's job at her company. She hadn't had much experience with interviewing, and hated putting people on the spot. Each time she asked someone why he or she wanted to work for the company, a little silence would fall and she'd jump in with, "I know this is hard but, you know, what do you think? I mean, why do you want to work here as opposed to somewhere else? Don't worry, it doesn't have to be anything really significant . . ."

She would rattle on until the people she was interviewing were as flustered as she was. They never had a chance to think about their answers because all their attention was on her. They wondered whether she was always this nervous, or whether she'd had too much coffee, or whether she was so put off by them that she didn't even want to hear their answers.

At the end of the day, Natalie said, "It's like pulling teeth to get these people to tell you anything."

Don't be concerned that they won't think you're a good conversationalist. That's not the point right now; the point is to find out what they want so that you have the information you need to propose action later on.

TECHNIQUE #30:
Go Slow to Go Fast

Don't rush the discussion or hurry the negotiation to a conclusion. Going too fast in the beginning can make people wary, suspicious, tense, and sometimes even panicky. If that happens, they may back out at the last minute and all your time and energy will be wasted.

Start out slowly, build trust, and everything will fall into place more quickly and easily in the long run. Any chef will tell you that the stir-fry is quicker and easier when the preparation—cutting and chopping—has been done in advance.

If you walk through life with a naturally quick pace, you may have a tendency to fly into a meeting (already knowing what you want), sit down, and get right to it. You may assume that everybody else has done his or her homework, too, and that they are all ready to have their say and make a decision.

If you are that kind of person, life can be very hard. Most people won't keep up with you. It may be torture for you to adapt to their slower pace, but you've probably already learned that sometimes you have to go slow to go fast later —especially when you are meeting people for the first time.

People don't like to be hurried. If they're suspicious because you want to wrap everything up immediately, you may have to start from scratch—with the disadvantage that they think you've already tried to put one over on them.

TECHNIQUE #31:
Ask Direct Questions

A wise man once said, "When all else fails, tell the truth."

With some people, you can be direct from the beginning. If you are connected, and the other person knows what he or she wants and feels confident about telling you what it is, then you are both lucky.

Other people need to be brought to this point with the techniques described earlier in this chapter. At some point, however, you may need to be direct and blunt. You may have to come right out and say, "Here's what I'm trying to do. I already know what I want, and I know you want something different. I have to know what you want in order for us to move toward something in the middle that will work for both of us. What exactly do you want?"

Seth was sales director at the greeting-card company Jackie owned. At his annual review, she offered him a big raise and was surprised when he didn't seem overjoyed. He thanked her, but slouched in his chair, looked at the floor, and acted hurt and upset.

"Seth, is something wrong?" she asked.

"No, I guess not," he said.

"Are you happy about the raise?"

"Oh, yeah!"

"Was there something else you wanted?" she asked.

"I don't know."

"What is it? What do you want?"

"Forget it."

"Seth, I'm not a mind reader here. I want to know what you want. Tell me!"

It turned out that Seth wanted to buy into the company, but mistakenly thought that Jackie wouldn't go for the idea.

Sometimes people need to be treated as children, especially if they are embarrassed to ask for what they want or don't think they can have it. Children need you to be very specific and direct, and sometimes adults do, too.

All of these techniques can help you play detective and find out what people want. As you practice, they become second nature and you're on your way to completing the first half of Part Two: Find out what they want.

EXERCISES

1. When was the last time a negotiation broke down because you didn't, or couldn't, find out what the other person wanted?
2. How could you have used each of the techniques in this chapter to put that interaction back on track?

ACCEPT WHERE THEY ARE

10

You can't raise positive people on negative
feedback.
—GERRY JAMPOLSKY, author of
Love Is Letting Go of Fear

Someone asks you what you want. You think about it and give
an honest answer, only to be attacked with a response like:

- "You're *kidding!*"
- "Oh, no! That would be a *disaster!*"
- "I used to think that, too."
- "Wait, you don't understand."
- "Do you know what you're *saying?!*"

How do these reactions make you feel? Most people close
down when battered with this kind of contempt, condescen-
sion, disgust, denial, or outright antagonism. They harden
their hearts, and either retreat entirely or arm themselves for
battle.

The second part of Step Two is "make them feel heard."
This doesn't mean "heard—and stupid or wrong"; it means
"heard—and respected."

For others to feel heard, you have to accept that they feel
the way they feel, and want what they want. They have to
know that you've seen their point of view and accept their

ideas as valid, even though they may be different from your own. They need to understand that you're not out to prove that you're right and they're wrong, but to find common ground.

It's only human for them to push back when they feel pushed. The more you resist them and their positions, the more they will resist you and your position. The more fully and clearly you accept where they are, the more flexible they will be.

TECHNIQUE #32:
Accept the Situation as It Is; Don't Pretend It's Something Different or Try to Make It What You Wish It Were

Remember, Steps One and Two are about finding out where the triangle's two base points are so that you can build a solid, stable foundation for the third point, your common ground.

Step One—Know exactly what you want—gives you the location of the first base point.

Step Two—Find out what they want and make them feel heard—tells you where the second base point is.

You need accurate information from Step One and Step Two in order to find a true third point that gives you lasting results. You need to know what people *really* want, not what you think they should want, what you wish they wanted, or what you hope they really mean.

People use two ploys to avoid accepting the situation as it is.

"You can't really want that; *you must mean* this . . ."

The words don't have to be spoken aloud; if you don't believe people when they tell you what they want, they'll know it. Their resistance will harden and they'll make it their business to *prove* it to you.

Denise was the crack account executive who had launched Amanda's advertising agency into the big time with an extraordinarily successful campaign for a national car rental service. Denise *was* the agency, and she knew it. Amanda knew that Denise would ask for the moon at her next salary review, and was not surprised when Denise requested a 100 percent raise. Amanda had looked at her own bottom line and decided that she would offer Denise a 60 percent raise and would go as high as 80 percent.

She was not prepared when Denise also asked to work at home. Amanda ran a tight ship and didn't like the idea that employees might be washing the dishes, gardening, or running errands on "her time," regardless of how much they did for the agency.

She had never worked at a place where people could work at home, had never considered it as an option for her employees, didn't like the idea, didn't even want to think about it, and simply could not accept that this was something that her star account exec wanted.

When Denise made the request, Amanda stared at her a moment, then gave a little laugh as if it were a joke and started talking about a 110 percent raise. Her own bottom line went out the window the minute she started dealing in hopes and fears, rather than in the realities of what Denise wanted.

Denise repeated her request and asked, "What do you think, Amanda? Can I do it or not?"

"You can't be serious," Amanda replied. "You'd miss out on all the interaction that goes on here, all the nuances, the give and take you need to do your job. You wouldn't like working at home. There'd be no stimulation, no excitement, no one to bounce ideas off of. You'd be crying for a desk back here in a week. Let's not confuse the issue with something you don't really want anyway."

Denise said, "I've thought about this quite a lot, and my priority right now is to be able to set my own hours and spend more time with my children. I guarantee the same quality of work and I'll probably be at my desk at four o'clock some mornings, but this is something I need in order to stay here."

She couldn't have been more direct, but Amanda still couldn't compute that this was essential to Denise. She stared at her blankly, said she'd have to think about it, and scheduled another time to finish the review.

Denise agreed to the meeting, but saw the writing on the

wall. She knew she wasn't being heard. That week she talked to two other agencies and one had no problem with the salary increase or with her working at home. When Amanda came back a week later still trying to hedge the issue, Denise quit.

She realized that if Amanda couldn't even accept that working at home was something she really wanted, there was no way she was going to get it. She gave up on the negotiation and, in her own self-interest, went looking for someone who could hear her.

"You'll change your mind when I tell you what's really going on . . ."

Again, the words don't actually have to be spoken for this condescending point of view to be understood.

Blake and Nick's innovative approach to efficiency planning included extensive interviews with employees at every level of the company, including the "lowliest" people in the typing pool.

James Bannon, who had founded the company forty years earlier and ran it with an iron fist, was appalled that these young kids might take some secretary's word over his and didn't want them poking around his domain. He'd only met with them because his son-in-law insisted, couldn't believe they'd even suggested these interviews, and was sure they'd change their minds when they saw how things really stood at the company.

"Let me tell you fellas how things work around here," he began. "We make all the decisions at the top. We're not in the habit of letting people whose last job was checking groceries tell us how to run a trucking business."

Blake and Nick gently tried to explain the purpose of the interviews and how their approach worked, but Bannon just kept telling them over and over "how things were."

They broke for lunch, and Blake said to Nick, "Hey, we're wasting our time here. We're hitting our heads against a brick wall. Even if we get this account, he won't like the results. Let's let this one go and put our energy where it'll do some good."

Bannon turned out to be "right" about those "kids" when they politely told him after lunch that their goals seemed incompatible, but he lost an opportunity to improve the company.

Ultimately, you have to deal with the reality of what people want, not what you think they should want or what you wish they wanted. You save time, energy, and perhaps even the relationship when you accept the situation *as it is* from the beginning.

TECHNIQUE #33:
Don't Let Emotional Reactions or Judgments About What They Want Sabotage the Negotiation

Most negotiations break down because of animosity between the two parties or a dislike of the situation, *not because of differences over issues*.

We all have a natural tendency to withdraw or to escalate the conflict when faced with people or ideas we find distasteful or threatening. The ability to manage your feelings, rather than letting them manage you, is more important than your ability to solve problems, and even more important than the issues being discussed.

If people's answers to Step Two press your hot buttons and you feel yourself starting to get angry, remember the triangle. Go back to Step One and use it to pull yourself out of the emotional tailspin by focusing on what you want.

Then remember that you can't do anything else until you finish Step Two. You have to find out what they want *and make them feel heard*—and you won't be able to listen if you're involved in your own emotional reaction. Just for now, pull yourself out of it, get centered, and give them your full attention.

You don't have to like them or their ideas; you only have to hear them, understand them, and accept that this is what they think. When you resist them, they only heat up and become *more* of whatever you don't like about them.

One of the most common emotional overreactions is some variation on: "*You want* what? *What kind of terrible person would want* that?"

Anita had been chosen by the five employees at Conrad's small dry-cleaning business to renegotiate their retirement benefits. Conrad wasn't a particularly diplomatic man and didn't feel well the day they sat down to talk. He began the negotiations by mumbling, "I'd like to give you all a twenty-dollar watch and make you disappear."

Anita was shocked. She had worked for this man for twenty-one years and, while their relationship had never been warm, she thought it was based on mutual respect and appreciation. She was hurt and angry, and felt tempted to hire a hungry young attorney who could and would negotiate tougher, more punishing terms than she was prepared to demand.

Anita steadied herself by going back to her bottom line. She was very clear about what she wanted: specific pension amounts and medical benefits, and also for everyone to come away from the table feeling good about one another and the agreement. She didn't want a few dollars more a month at the expense of a harmonious workplace and an easy working relationship with Conrad.

With this in mind, she put her knee-jerk emotional reaction aside and said to herself, "First of all, he may have been kidding or just grumpy. But even if that's what he really wants, I can understand it. He's close to retirement himself; why would he want to give us any more than he has to? This is a business, after all, not a support group. I know this man and he's not unreasonable; he knows he's going to have to give us more than we have now. Let's just take it from here, find out if this is what he really wants, and understand that we can probably come to some agreement without everybody going crazy. It's not going to do anybody any good for me to walk out in a huff, or to get all stony and angry."

She looked at him, smiled, and asked, "Can I have the Minnie Mouse watch?"

He laughed and said, "I'm sorry, Anita. I feel like hell. Tell me what you guys are gonna try to stick me for."

The rest of the talk went smoothly, and Anita got almost everything she requested.

Don't let other people, or your own emotional reactions, determine what you can or can't have in life. Remember that you need to know and accept what they want, whether or not you like what they say.

TECHNIQUE #34:
Avoid the Temptation to Talk Sooner, Higher, Faster, and Longer When You Feel Uncomfortable, Angry, or Threatened

Again, watch out for the fight-or-flight instinct. When we feel threatened or pressured, we tend to talk sooner, in a higher pitch, faster, and longer than normal—as if we're afraid that, if we let other people get a word in edgewise, we'll be even less likely to get what we want.

When you give in to this instinct and talk sooner, higher, faster, or longer, it closes down the communication and makes people less willing to talk about what they want. Fast speech, especially when it is high-pitched, tends to make people uncomfortable and defensive. A strident tone suggests tension and the desire to dominate. People literally feel they've been "fast-talked."

When you jump into the conversation and interrupt because you don't like what they are saying, other people don't feel they've had a chance to make their point. They may feel pressured and bullied; they certainly will not feel heard.

When you talk longer than is necessary, they feel you aren't interested in them, and want all the time, energy, and attention for yourself.

None of these reactions is helpful in a negotiation.

When you find yourself getting tense and reacting negatively to what others want:

1. Take a deep breath.
2. Recall your own bottom line, and get a mental picture of what you want.
3. Remember that you need that Step Two information, and that if you are upset with the other person, you probably aren't letting it in completely.
4. Plan ahead. If you don't listen to them, they won't listen to you—and you aren't listening to them if you're giving in to negative emotional reactions.
5. Let go of your negative emotional response so that you

can do what works: absorb the information and use it to move toward Step Three, proposing action in a way they can accept.
6. Make a conscious effort to wait until they're finished before you start to speak.
7. Pitch your voice low.
8. Speak slowly.
9. Be concise and to the point so that you don't talk too long.

TECHNIQUE #35:
Use the AAAA Approach to Create a Bridge Between You, Not a Gulf

When you are tempted to argue or disagree, ask more questions instead. Get more information, rather than escalating or withdrawing from the conflict.

Arguing creates a gulf; questions create a bridge. It is especially important to create this bridge *when you least feel like doing so*.

The AAAA Approach can guide you through this process:

- Acknowledge where they are. Listen actively, and let them know that you've heard what they said. Do this by paying close attention to what they say they want, and then:

  - repeating or paraphrasing it back to them using phrases like "I understand" or "I see."

- Ask for more information. Always use asking for more information as a substitute for argument. If you are upset or uncertain about what they want, or even if you just think they need to say it again, use phrases like:

  - "I think I understand, but would you mind running it by me once more?"

- "I'm not quite clear on the reasoning behind that. Could you go over it again, please?"
- "Could you explain this particular part of the proposal?"
- "Tell me again about that, if you would."

• Align with their needs and values. Listen for their real needs and values, and show that you share them.

- "I can see why that raise is important. I remember when our kids were growing up."
- "We've had to cut back, too, so I can appreciate your need for economy."
- "Our employees have voiced some of the same concerns, so I can see why you want them to have this."

• Add more information of your own. It's a way of keeping the negotiation open and continuing to talk until your positions get closer to one another. It also helps them understand your point of view and may give them some incentive to bend.

- "We refinanced our own loan this year; that's one reason we're particularly interested in this deal."
- "We've recently expanded to two new cities, so we're anxious to keep moving on this."

My client Cass used the AAAA technique in a difficult negotiation.

Arthur Thompson was proud of the chain of fourteen Mercury Office Supply stores he had founded across the Midwest and was selling them only reluctantly. His wife was quite ill and he was close to retirement, so they were going to move to Arizona for her health and to be closer to their children.

Arthur's asking price was a bit high, and Cass was only able to get funding for about 90 percent of it. She had worked in the office supply business for years and knew she could make the Mercury stores an even greater success, but Arthur refused to budge. He loved the business and couldn't see letting it go for a penny less than he was asking.

Cass had exhausted every possible source of funding and

knew her bottom line. Even if more money had been available, she thought that 90 percent of the asking price was fair and really couldn't afford to pay more. She knew she would do a better job with the business than the other potential buyer, and she knew that Arthur knew it as well. She couldn't understand why he was being so stubborn, and was quickly losing patience with him.

She wanted to pound on the desk and scream at him, "You idiot! Why are you making such a fuss? You want me to have it and I'm giving you everything I can!" Instead, she used the AAAA Approach.

1. She acknowledged where Arthur was by saying, "Arthur, I understand that this business means a lot to you, that you built it up from nothing with a lot of hard work and sacrifice, and that it's very dear to you. I hear that you don't want to let it go for ninety percent of what you're asking."

2. Then, instead of flying off the handle, she asked for more information about the business, about living in Arizona, about his plans for retirement, and then returned to more questions about the business. They hadn't been getting anywhere, but she didn't want the discussion to end. Asking questions kept their negotiation going, and also gave her more information—some of which she could use.

Still, Cass had a feeling that there was a piece missing from the picture of why Arthur wouldn't sell to her. She knew that he thought she was the best buyer, and that he would have plenty of money for his retirement regardless of whether he got 90 percent or 100 percent of the asking price. She finally decided to ask him directly.

"Arthur, I feel like I don't have all the pieces. We both know I'll do well by the business and that I want it badly. I know the money's important, but I have a feeling it's not all you care about. Why won't you sell to me?"

Her question pressed just the right button; an answer bubbled to the surface that surprised even Arthur. "When I started this business all I had was my Army back pay and a five-hundred-dollar loan from my father. I worked my fingers to the bone. I never saw my kids when they were growing up. My family went without so I could pour money back into the business. And then you come along and tell me it's not worth what I'm asking. Well I have news for you, miss. It's worth every penny of that price! I'm not going to give up everything my life's been about for ninety percent of what I want."

By the time he finished, he was practically yelling. Instead of letting her emotions take over and either shrinking back or getting defensive at his tirade, Cass was delighted. Now she had what she needed: the real reason that he wouldn't let her have the business. Arthur thought of the business as himself, as all the work and sacrifices he'd put into it, and her 90 percent offer seemed like a personal insult. It was a matter of pride for him not to give in to her.

Her first reaction was that this was silly, that it was typical of men to invest so much ego in a business, but she didn't let that judgment get in the way. She knew she was tired and frustrated by the negotiations, so she was particularly careful to steer clear of negative emotional reactions.

Instead, she thought back to what she wanted, which was to buy the business. Then she asked herself what would produce that result, and saw that it wouldn't work to give in to her own prejudices about his motivation. She had to accept Arthur's feelings and get on the same team with him. They had to be allies looking together for a solution to the problem, not adversaries. To do that, she had to validate his position again.

She played with her full deck. There was a part of her that greatly admired what Arthur had done, felt good about giving him credit, and wanted to carry on in the same tradition. That was the part she brought to the forefront.

3. She aligned with his needs and values and said, "I'm so glad you told me that, because now I understand your position better. I'd probably feel the same way if I'd done something as monumental as you have, and it's one reason I've always admired both you and the business. I'd like for us to find a way to acknowledge what you've done publicly so that other people can be inspired by it. I feel bad that I can't give you a hundred percent of the price. If I could, I would. I want to make sure you know that I'm only going down to ninety percent because that's all I can get and afford, not because I want to put anything over on you or in any way minimize what you've done."

When she was sure he'd received all that information, she went on to the next step.

4. She added more information of her own. She showed Arthur the bank's letters about her loans and gave him the figures she'd worked out to prove that she could only afford 90 percent. Then she added something else.

"Arthur, maybe I can make up that ten percent with an idea. I'd like to capitalize on the success of the Mercury name, but I'd also like for you to get the credit you deserve. Here's what I propose: I'd like to change the name of the stores to Mercury-Thompson, and to give away with each purchase a bookmark made of heavy stock that tells the story of how you founded Mercury and made it a success. I think it would be good for business, and it would make me feel good to acknowledge you in that way.

"I'd also like to hire you as a consultant for two years after the sale is final. I'd fly to Arizona twice a year to meet with you and get your input on what's happening, and I'd pay you a retainer."

Cass had said the magic words, and Arthur was delighted to sell to her. She reexperienced her victory each time she handed out one of those bookmarks.

Cass succeeded in this negotiation because she went to great lengths to find out exactly what Arthur wanted, to put aside her own emotional reactions and accept his position, and to make him feel heard in a tangible way.

Remember, you don't have to like what they want *or give it to them*. You only have to accept that this is what they want, to believe them, and to let them know that you have the information.

When you accept where people are, they feel heard and are more willing to answer more questions. When you put aside your own judgments and opinions of their wants, you avoid creating resistance in them or in yourself. The negotiation goes more quickly and smoothly, and everyone is more likely to get what he or she wants.

EXERCISES

1. The last time you were involved in a negotiation or solving a problem, did you honestly accept where others were and what they wanted? What was the result?
2. Imagine a situation in which you are asked for something that you consider outrageous. Think what the results would be if you accepted that this was what they wanted. Now think what the results would be if you resisted what they really wanted and created a counterresistance in them.

MAKE THEM FEEL HEARD

The opposite of a fact is a falsehood, but the opposite of one profound truth may very well be another profound truth.

—Niels Bohr

When people know on a gut level that you've heard what they want, you have completed Step Two. These are some techniques for making absolutely sure they know they've been heard.

TECHNIQUE #36:
Acknowledge Their Concerns

It can be uncomfortable to speak directly to people's problems and concerns. After all, these are what created the disagreement or made the negotiation necessary in the first place. They are the barriers and stumbling blocks, and it can be difficult to confront them directly.

It is also one of the most powerful things you can do. Acknowledging people's concerns—either by repeating them or by paraphrasing them—moves you forward in two important ways:

1. People know that if you can speak to these difficult issues, you have heard all the rest of what they've said and understood the core of their concerns. They also know that you aren't afraid to grapple with the real issues, and that you're genuinely interested in solving the problem.
2. When people feel that their concerns have been heard, those concerns tend to dissipate. When the problems aren't brought forward and acknowledged, they tend to grow and fester.

Suppose that the people with whom you are negotiating have told you that they are on a deadline and need to move quickly. You may have heard them, but they have no way of knowing that you're taking their concerns into account unless you say something like "I understand that we need to settle this quickly."

If they don't get this kind of reassurance, they may spend the rest of the negotiation wondering, "Did he understand what we said or is he fooling around? Does he know that we need to go fast with this? Does he *care?*"

This kind of second-guessing creates barriers between you, rather than bridges. They may be distracted from the discussion, fidgeting about whether you understand their problem and thinking that, if you don't, you may be working against their interests by not doing everything you can to speed things up.

All of this can be eliminated with a few words. If they know that you, too, are taking time into consideration, they can relax and work with you more easily.

Whatever their overriding interest, make sure they know that you heard their concerns and are taking them into account. If they are worried about economy, let them know that you understand by saying something like "We're all interested in saving money . . ."

If their primary concern is quality, say something like "We want to do this as quickly and economically as possible, but our number-one priority is to have the best product we can."

This way, everybody knows that you understand the problems, and you can go forward together.

TECHNIQUE #37:
Use Their Language

If you want people to know that you've heard what they said, you have to speak their language. Your responses have to reflect their values and their ideas—not yours.

When Rich presented the bid to paint Nat's house, Nat could tell that Rich considered himself a professional and that doing work of high quality was extremely important to him. He planned to use top-grade paints, had skilled people working for him, showed Nat pictures of other houses they'd painted, and was eager for Nat to call his references.

Nat wasn't sure he could afford to hire Rich and definitely intended to negotiate the price, but he wanted Rich to know that he'd heard what Rich said about the quality of his work. Nat said, "It sounds like your work is absolutely first-rate and that I'd be getting a top-quality, professional job."

He then went on to mention his own concern about how much he could afford just then, but the negotiation started on a cordial, mutually respectful note because Rich knew that Nat had heard him.

Gary and Jean both needed all their negotiating skills when he went in to ask her for a raise. She had figured out her bottom line before the meeting and was shocked at the vast difference between that bottom line and his request.

When she asked him how he'd come up with that figure, he said, "Jean, my wife and I haven't had a vacation in three years. She's frazzled and I'm burned out, but we can't afford to go away and pay someone to stay with the kids on what I make. I want a better life for us. We can't even go out to dinner."

Jean knew he needed more money, but she was very surprised at the reasons he gave and thought to herself, "Four kids to feed, clothe, entertain, and put through college . . . and you're worried about vacations and eating out?"

That's not what she said, however. Those thoughts reflected her values, not Gary's. For whatever reason, he was much more concerned at that point about sharing some leisure time with his wife. He probably wouldn't have felt heard if she'd said, "I know how expensive it is to raise kids today, and you probably want to put something aside for their schooling."

Instead, she said, "I understand. We all need to get away and relax. I wish I could be more helpful, Gary, but I have to be fair to the rest of the people here and what you're asking is way beyond what anyone else makes."

Gary's job was in sales, and he was no stranger to "make them feel heard" techniques. He spoke her language when he answered, "I know you want to be fair, Jean, and that's something I've always liked about working for you. But I have to be fair to myself and my family, too. I want to stay here. I like this place, but I have to have at least part of that raise. Maybe you and the boss could consider bringing everyone up a little."

It took some time for them to agree on Gary's raise, but the negotiation went as smoothly as could be expected because Gary and Jean each took the time to speak one another's language and to make sure that the other felt heard.

TECHNIQUE #38:
Avoid Emotional Terms That Imply Positive or Negative Reactions to What They Say

The point is simply to let them know that you heard them, not to suggest that you approve or disapprove of what they said. At this stage, any kind of judgment—positive or negative—could stall the negotiation or prolong the problem.

Some negative reactions to what people want are:

- "Oh, brother!"
- "Here we go again . . ."
- "You *always* say that."
- "You've got to be kidding. That's ridiculous!"

These responses invite others to escalate the conflict, and that's not what you want right now. You want people to stay open, tell you more, or listen to what you have to say.

If you convey a positive judgment, on the other hand, you run the risk that others will think you're trying to manipulate them—or that there really isn't any problem. "You're so right!" or "Just what I was thinking!" can sound smarmy. If you say "Terrific," "Exactly," or "I love it," they may ask, "So what's the problem? Let's do it my way if you agree!"

In any case, implying either a positive or a negative judgment throws the attention back on you, when it should be on them.

Your job is to provide them with a neutral, accepting, open environment in which to tell the truth about what they want and to make them feel heard. You'll get your turn later, and you're preparing the ground now for a positive response from them. Your patience and consideration will be well rewarded.

TECHNIQUE #39:
The More Intense the Conflict, the More Strongly and Explicitly You Must Acknowledge Their Position

If there is a great distance between you—either emotionally or in terms of your two positions—you may have to work harder to create a connection. One way to do this is to acknowledge what they say in strong and explicit terms.

If you already have a rapport with someone, he or she may feel completely heard if you simply make eye contact, smile, and say, "I see."

If the other person is antagonistic, you may have to paraphrase what he or she said, nod, lean forward, and use very definite and specific phrases like "I understand what you're saying."

Kathleen and Wally sold real estate loans for different branches of the same bank, and they had gotten into a dispute about territory. Wally believed that Kathleen was encroaching on his turf, so they both sat down with their boss, Theresa, to iron out the problem.

Kathleen had worked for the bank for seven years, and she and Theresa had become friends as well as colleagues. Wally was new to the job. Theresa was pleased to have him aboard because he was good at what he did, but she sensed that he disliked working for a woman and resented her position at the bank. Their personalities seemed like oil and water, and she found that he was far more pleasant to clients than he was to her.

When the three of them sat down, Theresa asked each of them what was going on. As Wally told his version of events, she leaned forward, nodded as he spoke, and said things like "I understand," "I hear what you're saying," and "I can see how that would be very upsetting."

She questioned him further about several details of Kathleen's "encroachment"—in a way that didn't threaten him, but only showed an interest in getting every detail of his story.

When he was through, she asked him whether there was anything else he wanted to say or get clear between himself and Kathleen. Then she said, "I want to thank you for telling me all that, Wally. I'm not sure how this is going to work out, but I'm sorry that the question even came up during your first few weeks. Your work has been excellent and I want things to go well for you here. I'm sure we'll come up with a solution that works for both of you."

Then she asked Kathleen to tell her version. Theresa's responses to her were far less dramatic. She trusted Kathleen, and Kathleen knew it. Their working relationship was on firm ground, and she didn't have to bend over backward to make Kathleen feel heard and acknowledged. She could tell Kathleen with a nod or a glance, "I understand everything you've said and I believe you."

The meeting resulted in a few new ground rules that made each person's territory clearer. Wally came away from the meeting feeling as if he'd scored a coup and might be able to work for Theresa after all. Kathleen understood exactly what had happened and didn't feel at all slighted. Wally's territory was actually a bit smaller and Kathleen and Theresa had weathered another storm together.

When you have found out what people want and made them feel heard, you have the two base points of the triangle in place and can start moving toward the third point—resolving the conflict or reaching the agreement with Step Three: "Propose action in a way they can accept."

EXERCISES

1. Recall the last time you did not feel heard in a negotiation. What was the result?
2. Remember a time that someone *did* make you feel heard. How did you feel and what happened in that negotiation?

STEP THREE:
Propose Action in a Way They Can Accept

SPEAK TO THEIR NEEDS FIRST

Slow down and the thing you are chasing will come around and catch you.

—Zen saying

You know what you want. You've found out what the other people want and made them feel heard. Now you can go on to Step Three: Propose action in a way they can accept. In this final Triangle Talk step, you discover the common ground between you and shape it into a solid agreement.

Step Three: Propose Action in a Way They Can Accept

People sometimes find it difficult to say what they want or make a proposal because they fear conflict or rejection.

When you use Triangle Talk, much of the potential conflict and rejection have already been defused through Steps One and Two. The clarity and confidence you gain from Step One set a calm, positive tone for your interaction. Others are more relaxed in your presence, so the connection between you comes more quickly and easily. As you explore what they want in Step Two, that connection deepens and their respect for you grows. Knowing that they've been heard makes them more willing to listen to your ideas, to negotiate openly, and to be flexible about finding solutions.

If you now put forward a fair proposal based on what you want and what they want, and if you present it in a way that speaks to their needs and values, you should walk away with a good agreement that makes everyone happy.

Show that you respect their position and are serious about the negotiation by developing a plan that will work for them. Don't give up what you want, but don't ask them to give up everything either. Then use the following techniques to propose it in a way they can accept.

TECHNIQUE #40:
Speak to Their Needs First

The top three complaints I hear from people in my seminars about their work environments are:

1. They don't think that people listen to them.
2. They don't feel respected.
3. They think that others try to control or manipulate them.

These three conditions are most likely to occur when you speak to your own needs first. They are least likely to occur when you speak first to other people's needs.

Most people are more interested in themselves than they are in you, and more interested in their own needs than in yours. Speaking first to what interests them most—their own needs—captures their attention, establishes a bond, and wins their trust and respect.

When you speak first to their needs, people—

• Start listening sooner.
• Pay more attention.
• Listen longer.
• Remember more of what you say.

- Have more respect for you.
- Think you are a more intelligent person, even a *better* person, so you deserve more latitude and freedom.
- Listen more closely when you talk about your own needs.

That's a pretty good return on the small investment of speaking to their needs first.

If you speak to your own needs first, on the other hand, people often tune out, get defensive, or escalate the conflict. They may stare back at you with glazed eyes and a stony expression, wondering whether you have any intention of considering their needs, and not hearing a word you say. This kind of fear and distrust can easily erupt into open hostility.

Colin went to see Linda about health insurance because the premium on his present policy had shot through the roof when he turned forty. He told her that he was self-employed, unable to pay a high premium, and just wanted to protect himself against a serious accident or illness. He was willing to accept a large deductible in order to get the lowest possible premium.

Linda pulled out her huge book of insurance programs and started reading, explaining the policies to Colin in great detail. After a few minutes, he became jumpy and irritable, almost angry. By the third policy, all he wanted was to get out of that room and never to see Linda again.

Linda made the most common Step Three mistake: she did not speak first to Colin's needs. From the minute she started talking, Colin was wondering, "Is she taking what I said into consideration at all, or is she going to read me that whole book? Is she looking for policies that are good for me, or good for her?"

In fact, Linda had heard exactly what Colin said, had gone directly to those policies that would best fulfill his needs, and was going to tell him about three of them and then let him choose—but Colin wasn't a mind reader, so he had no way of knowing that.

Linda could have eliminated the whole misunderstanding and won a loyal client if she had taken thirty seconds to say, "Let me see if I understand what you're looking for, Colin. You want the lowest possible premium, with general coverage for major catastrophes, and you're willing to go with a higher deductible. Did I miss anything, or shall we go ahead in that direction?"

If he'd agreed, she could have said, "I have three plans that I think will suit your needs. Why don't I go over each of them and then answer any questions you have?"

Remember that people are usually anxious at the beginning of a conflict or negotiation. Anything you can do to calm their fears will make the situation easier and more productive for everyone. When you speak to their needs first, you reassure them that your proposal takes their concerns into account, and they can relax on that score.

Speaking to their needs first also puts you on the same team. You are working together, aligned against the problem rather than against one another.

Why We Usually Speak to Our Own Needs First

People usually speak to their own needs first because:

1. They don't know what those needs are and hope that the answers will emerge as they "talk it through"—a process that should be done with colleagues or in private, not during the negotiation itself, or
2. They are afraid they can't have what they want and are trying to muscle their agenda through by aggression, coercion, talking more, and talking louder, or
3. Both of the above.

When we're not sure what we want, it's almost impossible to care about or speak to what others want. We sense that we're at a disadvantage, and are inclined to be defensive.

Janet had advertised her car for "$3,000 or best offer," but in fact she didn't know much about selling used cars, wasn't clear on her real bottom line, and was afraid of being cheated. Ned told her that he just wanted the car for commuting to work—he had an RV for longer travel and camping trips— and offered her $2,300.

Instead of speaking first to his needs—talking about how she'd used the car for commuting, too, and had gotten excellent mileage in the city—she started thinking out loud, stalling for time, and trying to figure out whether she would accept his offer. She didn't know exactly why she needed more time, except that if the sale hadn't happened yet, she hadn't been cheated yet.

She went on and on about the new tires she had bought a year ago, the clutch she'd replaced, the low mileage, the big down payment on the new car, her incredibly high income taxes, and the fact that she had a child starting college the next fall.

Ned was mystified and put off. He thought he'd been pretty clear: he'd offered $2,300. Was that the "best offer" or not? He could see the low mileage and new tires. Who cared about her income taxes? A child starting college? These weren't his problems. Finally he gave her his number and asked her to call him if she didn't get any better offers. By the time she called him back, he had bought another car.

Ned and Janet might not have struck a deal even if she had spoken first to his needs, but whatever chance they had evaporated when she spoke first to hers. It left them no room to negotiate.

Speaking first to others' needs is one of the simplest, most powerful tools at your disposal. It requires a little more forethought, but it costs you nothing, takes very little time, and almost always enhances the negotiation.

TECHNIQUE #41:
"Bridge" from Their Interests to Your Common Interests to Your Interests

"Bridging" lets you work around to talking about your interests via the path that is most interesting and appealing to others: their interests, and the interests you have in common. People are almost always more open and receptive when you speak to the issues in this order:

1. Their interests.
2. Your common ground or common interests.
3. Your interests.

Begin with their favorite subject: what they want. Speak about the parts of what they want that are most like what *you* want, and then move on to what you *both* want. Then bridge into your own agenda. The progression is smooth and natural, and everything you say is connected in one way or another to their needs.

Bridging can be done quickly, easily, and effortlessly:

- "I understand that you feel our first concern should be cost-effectiveness (their idea), and I agree (the common ground). I've found a new design that's in line with that priority (your idea)."
- "Holding the seminar out of town (their idea) has created a lot of enthusiasm (common ground). I'd like to tell you about one place in particular that I'd recommend (your idea)."

You're "going slow to go fast." Even when bridging is a longer process, all you have to remember is the simple progression: their ideas, to the common ground, to your ideas.

Shirley worked for a large beverage company with offices all over the country. The promotion she was offered would take her to St. Louis, but she much preferred to remain in Chicago. She was sure she could do the job just as well from Chicago with her computer and two or three short trips a month to St. Louis.

Her new boss voiced several objections, but agreed to meet with her to discuss it. She had written him a letter stating her case for doing the job from Chicago, but when they actually sat down, that's not where she began. Instead, she started by talking about his objections.

"Bruce, I've thought a lot about your concerns . . ." She paraphrased many of the objections he'd mentioned earlier and asked him if he had any more, paying close attention to his answers.

She made sure Bruce knew that she understood and shared his concerns; then she bridged to their common interest. They shared the same top priority—both wanted Shirley to succeed at her new position—and she convinced him that she wouldn't sacrifice an ounce of effectiveness if she stayed in Chicago.

From their common ground, she bridged to the solutions she had worked out. She detailed how she could guarantee the same high level of performance from Chicago as she could from St. Louis.

In the end, Shirley got to stay in Chicago. She and Bruce agreed to meet again in six months to evaluate how the arrangement was working, and that first encounter set a positive tone for their future working relationship.

Shirley kept Bruce's attention and goodwill, and prevented the situation from becoming adversarial, by bridging from—

1. *Bruce's interests* (his concern that she couldn't do a good job from Chicago), to
2. *their common interests* (that she do a good job), to
3. *her interests* (why she could do a good job from Chicago).

Speaking first to other people's needs builds a foundation of trust, respect, and liking on which to base everything else you say.

EXERCISES

1. The last time you found yourself in a difficult situation, did you speak first to the other person's needs? If you didn't, what could you have said?
2. Recall the last time someone spoke first to his or her own needs. How did you feel?
3. Can you recall the last time someone spoke first to your needs? If you can, how did it make you feel?

POSITION YOURSELF AND YOUR IDEAS

The power to define is the power to choose.
—MICHAEL O'NEAL

Positioning means establishing and defining how people see something: you, your proposal, a situation, a relationship. Jack Trout and Al Ries popularized this concept as a marketing technique in their book *Positioning*, and it is the key to success in Step Three.

When you position your proposal well, you accomplish three important things:

1. You show people what's in it for them. Speaking about your ideas in terms of their value to others shows people that it is more to their advantage to be with you than against you.
2. You let others know that you are interested in collaboration, not competition, and that your intentions are decent and honorable.
3. You shift the attention away from their fears and toward the opportunities that your proposal affords them.

Whoever most vividly characterizes what a situation is about usually determines how others—

- Perceive it.
- Think about it.
- Talk about it.
- Decide on it.

The techniques in this chapter offer ways to position your ideas so that others find them easy to accept.

TECHNIQUE #42:
Paint Them a Colorful, Detailed Picture

Bright, vivid verbal snapshots make people remember what you say. When you create a striking word picture of the result you want, that is the image people carry in their minds. They see your ideas the way you want them to be seen.

Less effective: "I think we should build a thirty-story office building downtown."

More effective: "I see a shining tower rising above our city, windows flashing in the sunlight, a place that will make people remember our work, and that we can be proud of each morning as we ride up to the plush penthouse suite."

Less effective: "I want to come to work for you."

More effective: "Mr. Jones, I can see myself marching through that door each morning with a smile on my face, eager to get at the things we've just been talking about. If you give me this chance, I'll make you a star in six months."

Less effective: "I believe this campaign will appeal to young people."

More effective: "Kids will wake up with this jingle ringing in their ears and race downstairs for a tall stack of these rich, delicious pancakes dripping in maple syrup."

TECHNIQUE #43:
Align with Their Personal or Organizational Values

People are more relaxed, trusting, and open to your ideas when they know that you share the same personal or organizational values. Shared personal values might include religion, family, philosophy of life, or leisure interests. Shared organizational values include whatever qualities are encouraged and rewarded in their particular organizational culture. These might be loyalty, the bottom line, moving up the ladder, communication, or employee input into decision-making.

Shared values put you on the same team and create more room for give and take in the relationship.

The Cardinal was trying to get Patrick O'Donahue to build the new convent at a fraction of what he would normally charge. The charming O'Donahue had been a loyal parishioner for thirty years and wanted to give the sisters a break, but he didn't want to lose his shirt in the process.

He knew that the Cardinal was the son of a bricklayer and a big supporter of labor, so O'Donahue began with a smile, "Your Eminence, I agree that we should do all we can for the good sisters, and you know that nothing gives me more pleasure than contributing what I can to the church. What worries me just a bit is how to balance the sisters' needs with the needs of my hardworking men. Now, I don't feel quite right asking them to work for free or take pay cuts so that we can build the convent for what you're proposing, and I wonder if we can find a figure that comes out right both for my men and for the sisters."

O'Donahue aligned with the Cardinal's personal values (labor) and his organizational values (parishioners should contribute to the church according to their means) before he made his proposal. He put himself and the Cardinal on the same team, working together for the sisters and the workers against the high cost of building.

TECHNIQUE #44:
Position Your Proposal with "Social Proof," Authoritative Endorsements, Likability, and Appeals to Others' Self-Images

Whenever you try to reach an agreement or solve a problem, you are asking people to change. People do not like to change, even when they are in deep personal pain. It is human nature to resist change of any kind—even when the present situation is painful or the change is good change. Moving to a new house is difficult, even when it is a nicer house. Starting a new job is uncomfortable, even when it is a promotion.

Good negotiators go out of their way to make change easier for others. The best way to do this is to demonstrate that the change you are requesting is an *extension* and *expansion* of who they are and what they've done, not an *alteration* or *invalidation* of themselves or their past actions.

Change is also less difficult for people when—

- Others whom they admire have made the same change.
- People in authority endorse the idea.
- They believe that you like them or *are* like them.
- You appeal to their image of themselves.

Social Proof

Russ learned how "social proof" worked when he went up and down Main Street selling ads for his high-school yearbook. He told each merchant about others who had already bought space in the yearbook, and this worked well for the most part. People felt better knowing that they weren't the only ones on the street who had bought ads.

Only once did this technique backfire on Russ. He told the owner of a shop that sold matronly dresses that Hotlines, a trendy store two blocks away stocked with outrageous fashions for teenagers, had bought an ad. The older woman sniffed and practically threw him out of her shop.

Be careful who and what you use as social proof. You may

think someone or something is terrific, but the person to whom you're talking may not. Don't assume you know what other people's values are, or whom they admire. Take the time to investigate first, and go slowly if you aren't sure.

Places and behaviors can also be used to establish social proof:

- Places:
    - "Oh, I'm from Portland, too" establishes a bond.
    - "This is what they're doing in New York now" suggests that it is the most effective method.
    - "The style in Paris is . . ." lends an aura of fashion legitimacy.
- Behaviors:
    - Government officials often use the same mannerisms, body language, and speech patterns as the President in a conscious or unconscious attempt to be perceived as more powerful.
    - Giving a thumbs-up makes people think of astronauts and test pilots, just as high fives make them think of professional athletes.

Authoritative Endorsement

Experts, celebrities, authorities, and heroes inspire credibility and trust. People find change easier if someone well known or in authority has already done what you suggest doing.

- Endorsements from star athletes sell millions of dollars worth of shoes and other sports equipment.
- Political candidates court endorsements from better-known or more popular figures in their party.

Likability

People like, trust, and feel most comfortable with people who *like* them, and with people who *are* like them.

Bring forward those qualities in yourself that are most like the qualities of others, and remember the old saying: "People don't care what you know until they know that you care."

Don't hesitate to voice your genuine admiration for the people with whom you are negotiating, or for people who are like them or share their values.

If your new boss values the team approach, is detail-oriented, and likes problems to be solved from the bottom up, concentrate on those qualities when she asks your opinions of the work group. Mention that you enjoy the group's ability to pull together. Daniel, for example, never lets details fall through the cracks—and the group members pride themselves on being able to talk to one another and iron out difficulties.

Appeal to Others' Self-Image

We all have an image of ourselves based on our past experiences and on who we hope we are. Many of our decisions are made either to protect this self-image or to enhance it.

When people believe that your ideas affirm or enhance their self-image, they are more open to your proposal.

Nine-year-old Gloria learned this lesson selling Girl Scout cookies. The troop leader knew Gloria was marked for greatness after the little girl met with Henry Berger, who owned a twenty-story downtown office building. Berger was very strict about not letting anyone solicit inside the building, but could hardly turn down Gloria when she asked to meet with him in his penthouse suite.

She came dressed in her Scout uniform and armed with samples of cookies. She said she knew he never allowed people to set up tables and sell things inside the building's main entrance, but her mother had told her that he was a very important man and had done a lot of good for the people in their town, especially the children.

She asked if he knew about the Scout youth programs and told some touching stories about herself and other Scouts who had benefited from them. Then she appealed again to his self-image as a civic leader and philanthropist. "I hope you'll make an exception for us, Mr. Berger, because now you know that we're the good kind of program that you always support."

Within thirty minutes, Gloria had extracted permission to set up a table inside the entrance from four to six for three days the following week—and Berger had purchased six boxes of cookies.

TECHNIQUE #45:
Give Something Away Up Front, Without Being Asked

When you give a gift, people instinctively want to reciprocate. Giving something away may mean anything from conceding a point of the negotiation to offering a drink at the beginning of a meeting.

If you give people something up front, before you are asked to do so, they may consciously or unconsciously feel that they owe you something—even if it is only a little more listening and consideration.

This principle was illustrated in a study in which certain products were presented under three sets of circumstances. The first group was served coffee, tea, and juices from a silver platter during the presentation. They were the most likely to buy the products. The second group was offered the same refreshments on tin service trays, and they were less likely to buy. The third group was offered no refreshments at all, and bought the least.

TECHNIQUE #46:
Sandwich Your Controversial or Bad News Between Two Pieces of Good News

We all have to discuss controversial or negative issues from time to time. When you have to be the bearer of bad news, sandwich your unwelcome information between two pieces of good news. This softens the blow and prevents people from associating the bad news with *you*.

For example, you may convince your tight-fisted supervisor

to pay for a stress-management program for your staff by saying:

(Positive sandwich step) "I'm happy to report that our department has exceeded our production schedule this year.

(The bad news) "And because we've worked so hard, several members of my staff are experiencing burnout. I know you thought our last stress-management program was expensive and didn't help much, so . . .

(Positive sandwich step) "I've found several stress-reduction consultants who have excellent credentials and can be flexible on price."

You can also use this sandwiching technique when you have to give input that might be interpreted as negative. Suppose you joined the company six months ago and your boss asks your perspective on its direction and management. Your experience is generally positive, but you see enough problems that "Oh, everything's great" wouldn't be entirely accurate, and you believe that your boss wants your honest opinion. You might:

(Positive sandwich step) Say how much you enjoy working there, and single out a few specific projects that have been particularly enjoyable and instructive.

(The bad news) Mention that you are concerned about some possible problems on the horizon and ask, "May I talk with you about them?" (When you want people to stay open to your ideas, or when you want to bring their attention back to what you are saying, ask their permission to proceed.) Then frame your comments not as complaints, but as the concerns of someone who supports the company's success.

(Positive sandwich step) Then go on to thank your boss for hearing you out, tell him or her you've thought about some solutions, and ask permission to explore those ideas with him or her.

Sandwiching also works when someone asks you to explain a conflict you've had with a third person:

(Positive sandwich step) First characterize the difficult person's strong suit in your relationship, the things you admire about that person and the qualities you consider positive.

(The bad news) Describe the conflict in factual, nonemotional terms and tone.

(Positive sandwich step) Then talk about something good that

has happened as a result of the conflict, or some way in which the relationship has been healed.

Sandwiching is an excellent way to Teflon-coat yourself with two pieces of good news and avoid being associated with any bad news you may have to report.

TECHNIQUE #47:
Choose Your Point of Emphasis

The same information can be presented in many different ways; which points you choose to emphasize will radically affect how that information is received.

The chain-smoking priest asked his bishop, "May I smoke while I pray?"

The bishop replied indignantly, "Of course not!"

If he had thought to choose his point of emphasis, the priest might have asked, "Would you mind if I prayed while I smoked?"

Choosing the point of emphasis can determine not only the *way* issues are discussed, but even which issues are discussed and which are not. The issues of the 1988 presidential election were selected by candidate George Bush, whose skilled speechwriter, Peggy Noonan, gave him the memorable phrases "a thousand points of light," "a kinder, gentler nation," and "Read my lips. No new taxes."

By establishing the most vivid points of emphasis, Noonan helped Bush determine the playing field on which the campaign was fought. As he discovered, this is a key advantage in any negotiation or conflict.

TECHNIQUE #48:
Lavish "Velcro Praise" on Others

When you praise specific qualities in others, those same qualities rub off on you—and they stick. If you say that someone is efficient, for instance, people will perceive *you* as efficient.

President Bush mastered this technique as well. In his 1988 televised debates with Democratic candidate Michael Dukakis, a reporter asked the future President, "You have consistently attacked Governor Dukakis. Isn't there something positive you can say about him?"

Bush turned to Dukakis with a warm grin spreading over his face, then looked back to the reporter, and then straight into the camera as he responded, "You know, Barbara and I were discussing that just the other day. We were watching the Democratic convention on TV and there was that very special moment when Kitty Dukakis and the rest of his lovely family joined him on the platform. It was very clear to us that they were a strong and loving and very committed family."

Immediately, the American public perceived Bush as a dedicated family man.

The camera panned to Dukakis, whose face was drawn into a tight smile. The reporter asked Dukakis the same question and he shot back, "Well, at least he didn't call 'em the 'L' word [Liberal]." Dukakis lost a golden opportunity to lavish some "Velcro praise" on Bush and leave the impression that he shared those same wonderful qualities.

This principle works in reverse as well. Another politician, Adlai Stevenson, once said, "If you throw mud, you get dirty." When you talk about others' negative qualities, they become yours as well.

TECHNIQUE #49:
Make Sharp Contrasts

Your ideas always look better after people have been shown an undesirable alternative. Real estate agents often show clients several "dogs"—run-down, unattractive, or otherwise unappealing houses—before taking them to see the house they want them to buy. That house may be mediocre, but it looks fantastic next to the "dogs."

Use sharp contrast to position your proposal by presenting:

- The worst-case scenario before your best-case proposal: "If we go forward with these pay hikes, it is virtually certain that the company will go bankrupt. By keeping wages steady, we can survive the crisis and may be able to give raises next year."
- An extremely uncomfortable alternative before your more comfortable one: "We've considered the possibility of raising association membership by one hundred dollars, but now believe that we can get by if we raise it only sixty dollars annually."
- A possible threat before your opportunity: "If the drought continues, we could face steeper water rationing and be down to 25 percent of what we used five years ago. Our desalination plant involves a large initial investment, but would give us an almost unlimited supply of water and could actually save money in the long run."

TECHNIQUE #50:
Move from the Larger to the Smaller Picture

If you want others to do, buy, or participate more than they had planned to do, begin with the deluxe option, one that is much larger or more extravagant than what they had originally envisioned. Then offer a slightly more bare-bones alternative. Finally, fall back to an alternative that is even further reduced, but still more than what they had first thought they would be doing, buying, or participating in.

Here's how a salesman named Eric used this principle to sell Abe a suit. Abe wasn't a clotheshorse and didn't want to spend a great deal of money, but he did recognize the value of good appearance in his work. He planned on spending $350 for a conservatively tailored suit that would be appropriate for most occasions and seasons.

When Abe stepped into the store, Eric brought forth his array of Triangle Talk techniques. He didn't ask Abe a yes or no question like "May I help you?" which could have closed the door if Abe had said, "No, thanks." Instead, Eric acknowledged Abe's presence, went slow to go fast later, and used an open, Columbo-style greeting: "Hello. I hope you enjoy shopping in our store. I'm available if you have any questions."

This introduction made him approachable, and Abe told Eric he was looking for a suit. Eric asked a few questions, then said, "Let's try on a few to see what styles and colors are best for you."

The first suit made Abe look terrific. His slight paunch disappeared as if by magic; the tailoring made Abe look the way he'd always dreamed of looking—and no wonder, because the price tag read $1,300! This was way beyond what he'd had in mind. Eric understood completely and brought Abe another suit. Abe stepped back to the three-way mirror and saw that this suit was almost as stunning as the first, but that the price was $900.

Next, Eric had Abe try on a $650 suit, and that slight bulge around his middle started to show for the first time. Abe bought the next suit he tried on, which after all was only $420.

Eric then moved closer to Abe and appeared to notice his shirt for the first time. He discreetly suggested that Abe might want to have (not "buy") a shirt that would go with his new suit. Before Abe left the store, he had purchased a suit that cost $70 more than he had intended to pay, two expensive shirts, a tie, and a belt.

Abe was delighted with his purchases, which looked great on him and were an excellent investment. Eric thought as he rang up the sale, "Larger, then smaller."

TECHNIQUE #51:
Remember the Two-Choice Rule

When you want people to make a choice quickly, offer them two alternatives, either of which would be comfortable for you. They are more likely to reach a decision *now* when offered two alternatives, and making this choice both builds momentum toward reaching the agreement and restarts a discussion that has stalled.

The other advantage is that even if neither alternative is exactly what people want, they may feel better if they at least have a choice between two options and can name their own poison.

- "We can raise dues by ten percent or twenty percent. You choose."
- "I'm sorry to saddle you with this report so late in the week. Would you rather give it to me Friday and have the weekend free, or wait until Monday morning?"

TECHNIQUE #52:
Use the Rule of Scarcity

People are more likely to want something, and to make a decision about it *now*, if there is some form of scarcity associated with it. The scarcity may involve time, quantity, quality—anything that suggests that they won't be able to have this particular item or agreement unless they take it now:

- "We only have until four o'clock this afternoon. At that point, we're going to take the best offer we have."
- "We only have two of these models left and don't know if we can reorder."
- "There are copies, of course, but this is the only original."

If you are selling your car through a newspaper ad, ask callers if they'd like the nine-twenty or the nine-thirty appointment. They will envision lines of potential buyers winding around your block and reason: (1) This car must be a fantastic deal, and (2) They had better jump in quickly or someone else will snap it up.

People are afraid of missing out on something that is rare or won't be available forever. If there is any element of scarcity involved in what you are proposing, make sure they know about it.

It simply makes sense to position your proposal in the best

possible light. Remember, Step Three is about proposing action *in a way they can accept*.

EXERCISES

1. Think of an agreement you're now in the process of reaching, or a problem you are attempting to solve. Which of these positioning techniques can you use to present it *in a way people can accept?*
2. Recall the last time you made a proposal. Which of these techniques did you use? Which did you not use that might have been valuable?

OVERCOME OBSTACLES I: Staying Connected When the Going Gets Tough

Men's actions depend to a great extent upon fear
of loss.

—JOHN MILHOURN

Step Three takes you down to the wire. Everyone must finally
decide what they will and will not accept, so this is the place
where obstacles are most likely to surface.

For "obstacles," you can usually read "trouble between people." Remember, the issues being discussed are rarely as important as the relationships, or lack thereof, between
individuals.

The key to overcoming obstacles is *staying connected with the
people who seem to be the problem*, especially when all you want
to do is smack them hard and stalk out the door. If that
connection is broken, you may never get it back. You may
lose not only a successful negotiation, but a chance to become
a bigger person.

The secret to staying connected with others in difficult situations is to remember that *it's not their fault, and it's not your
fault; it's simply that this particular situation, at this particular time,
has pressed some hot buttons.*

For whatever reasons—unresolved internal issues, seeing
parts of ourselves we don't like, being reminded of people

from the past with whom we had trouble—the "oil and water factor" has come into play.

In Step One, you looked at your own panel of hot buttons. In Step Two, you learned to research and work with others' hot buttons. Now we'll look at what happens when you're together, in the middle of the negotiation, and everybody's hot buttons start lighting up.

Remember, the three main benefits of learning to identify and deactivate these hot buttons are:

1. You learn about yourself, and so you grow.
2. You can set your own course; you don't let somebody else determine your behavior.
3. You become a calmer, stronger, and more effective person and negotiator.

Staying connected is more difficult when others are playing by different rules. They may insist that the problem is really *you* and refuse to examine their own hot buttons. When this happens, bite the bullet and take the high road for the sake of your own integrity and your own results. You may not get any credit for being the more responsible "adult" and holding the negotiation together, but you will get a good agreement —and no one can take that away from you.

Our instincts are to protect and defend in the face of conflict. It takes practice to open up and embrace conflict, examine the lessons it may teach us, and stay connected to others.

This chapter is about keeping and strengthening those connections, even when you disagree, when you are angry, or when your needs seem directly opposed.

When the going gets tough, the tough stay connected.

TECHNIQUE #53:
Let Conflict Surface When It Exists, but Keep
It Under Control and Don't Dig In Your Heels

This technique keeps you balanced between those two primitive instincts, fight and flight. You don't withdraw from the
conflict, nor do you let it escalate out of proportion.

Some people are inclined to withdraw. They tend to look
victimized and to invite attack by others. This gets them even
more deeply enmeshed in the conflict. The problem sticks to
them like flypaper, disrupting their peace of mind and poi-
soning their interactions with everyone involved.

They don't want to let the conflict surface because—

1. Talking about it might make it more real.
2. The other person might get angry or go away.
3. They hope it will just disappear.

In fact, just the opposite is true:

1. The problem is real, whether or not it is discussed. The
   longer it is *not* discussed, the bigger it gets.
2. The relationship is at *greater* risk if the problem isn't
   handled. Unacknowledged conflicts drive wedges between people; working out difficulties brings them
   together.
3. Conflicts almost never go away of their own accord; they
   only keep popping up in different forms.

You can't deal with problems that you can't see and can't
talk about. When trouble is left to simmer on the back burner,
it eventually boils over. Then you have to deal with it in an
aggravated form, and often when you are in an agitated state.

The first step to solving a problem is to air it openly.

Heather had gained fifteen pounds her first year under
contract with Arlene's modeling agency. The word was that
Arlene simply did not renew the contracts of women who had

gained that much weight, and it was the last thing Heather wanted to discuss when they sat down to talk about her future. Instead, she talked—as fast as she could—about working harder, developing some new looks, and giving the agency a bigger cut.

No matter what she said, however, or how fast she talked, that fifteen pounds loomed as an unacknowledged barrier between Heather and Arlene. It didn't go away simply because Heather refused to address it. Arlene had no reason to address it; she had twenty aspiring models waiting in the wings and no inclination to shepherd Heather through a weight problem. Arlene finally told her gently but firmly that they were cutting back and couldn't renew her contract.

By ignoring the problem, Heather never solved it. Arlene might not have renewed the contract in any case, but Heather would have had a better chance if she had dealt with the fifteen pounds directly. She could have told Arlene that she knew she had to get rid of the extra pounds and outlined her plan for doing so. She could have indicated her good faith by suggesting a date by which she agreed to lose the weight and offering to insert a clause in the contract that ended their agreement if she failed to achieve that goal.

By meeting the problem head-on, she could have left the meeting with a contract, and Arlene could have left with assurances that one of her top models would soon be bookable again.

When you are the one who takes the initiative and brings a problem out into the open, you can choose the timing, the circumstances, and the framework in which you discuss it. If Arlene had brought up the fifteen pounds, it would have been discussed as a problem. If Heather had brought it up, she could have made sure it was discussed in terms of solutions.

Set Limits

Allowing conflict to surface doesn't mean letting the discussion turn into a free-for-all. You may have to set some boundaries and limits. These are some perimeters you may want to consider:

Are there any ground rules? This might include no yelling, no interrupting, and no physical violence.

What are the limits on subject matter? If the discussion is about renewing a contract, for instance, can issues that arose before the last renewal be brought up? If you are discussing one item on an agenda, can people bring up other items or must those subjects wait their turn?

Avoid Letting Positions Harden

It's also important to let conflict surface in ways that don't polarize people. The same conflict can be brought up in a neutral way, or in a way that actually aggravates it.

Neutral: "There seem to be some differences for us to work out."

Polarizing: "Well, obviously your side feels one way and our side feels another, and we're going to have to fight this out."

Five other techniques for preventing hardening of the positions, especially when you are negotiating major issues with many people involved, are the following:

1. Decrease the amount of direct interaction in the early stages of mediation. It's best if the principals don't go head-to-head during the first, and sometimes most difficult, stages of a negotiation. This is why the Secretary of State meets with foreign ministers before a summit conference to set the agenda, clear out the most difficult issues, and decide many points before the President ever sits down with the other head of state.
2. Decrease the amount of time between problem-solving sessions. This keeps the momentum going toward resolution and minimizes the tendency to go back to allies, pick apart the other side's position, and develop an adversarial frame of mind.
3. Decrease formality. Instead of sitting on opposite sides of a conference table dressed in dark suits and reading one another their position papers, people may need to loosen their ties, have lunch together, and talk.
4. Limit how widely, and how far back historically, prec-

edents can be cited. Can you go back to the beginning of the company and open the floor to such comments as "Well, it worked fine in 1932!" If a certain strategy worked for a carpet manufacturer, can it be used to make a point about your software business?

5. Use mediators, especially if the conflict is continuing or you don't seem to be getting anywhere. A third party whose job it is to move both of you toward resolution —not to represent one or the other position—can bring new energy and perspective to the negotiation.

One thing is certain: Conflict *will surface*, and it will be more manageable if you choose the time, place, and circumstances under which it is discussed.

TECHNIQUE #54:
Remember That the Problem Is Not the Other Person; It's How You React to One Another in the Situation

The answer is not to change other people or to make them the bad guys. The more you resist others or try to change their behavior, the more they act the way that makes you crazy. Have you ever noticed how, when you tell someone he's a jerk, he goes out of his way to prove you right?

When the situation heats up, use these four steps to take back control and use what is happening to your advantage:

1. Remind yourself that nobody is right or wrong; it's just that people are pushing your hot buttons—and you may be pushing theirs.

2. Remember that you may have to be the one to pull back, cool down, and deal with the situation. You can't count on others to understand what is happening or to recognize their own hot buttons, let alone yours. If you want the results, you have to go for them unilaterally. If you wait for others, it may never happen.

3. Ask yourself which hot button is being pressed, so that you understand why you are reacting so strongly and can let go. We will explore this process more fully in the next chapter.

4. Ask yourself what you can learn from the person or the situation. This lets you transform the differences between you from a liability into an asset. People who are different from you can teach you about parts of yourself that are as yet undeveloped.

Brian and Grace were always at each other's throats because he was task-oriented and she was people-oriented. They had worked together for about a year when Brian decided to turn the situation around.

He didn't really believe in this hot button business. He simply thought he was effective and Grace wasn't, and that she tried to cover her tracks by being nice. He was sick of the conflict, however, and decided to give this technique a try.

First, he reminded himself that nobody was right or wrong. In the beginning, he had to *act as if* the problem wasn't really Grace, and let go of the idea that the conflict was all her fault.

Second, he forced himself to stop thinking, "Why should *I* do anything about it if *she* doesn't?" He told himself that he had to act unilaterally. Grace simply wasn't going to deal with the issue; if he wanted anything done about it, he had to do it himself.

Third, he had to deal with the difficult issue of hot buttons. He had to pretend—even to himself—that his anger was just a reaction to some earlier fear, childhood incident, or unresolved part of himself. When he did this, he was surprised to notice that an incident actually did come to mind. When he was ten, his father had caught him goofing around with friends instead of "getting the job done" by mowing the lawn, and had punished him severely.

Fourth, Brian asked himself, "What can I learn from this situation?" He had already learned something about himself—one reason that he was inclined to be task-oriented—and he also realized that he could let Grace show him how to be more relaxed and enjoy people more, perhaps even get more done because he was connected to them.

Adopting this new perspective and doing this internal work allowed Brian to turn around his relationship with Grace. She no longer controlled how he felt or what kind of day he had. He was much more relaxed and productive around her, and his new attitude made her less antagonistic as well. She even began to ask his help and advice on some projects, and seemed to accept and appreciate his way of doing things more.

Brian kept using this technique despite the discomfort because it worked—and he was more interested in getting results than he was in being right.

TECHNIQUE #55:
Remember That You Always Have Only Three Choices: (1) Accept the Situation; (2) Leave; or (3) Change Your Behavior

Sooner or later, you always have to do one of these three things. You often experience the greatest anger, fear, or irritation when you stand between choices, frozen in the middle. The longer you wait before deciding, the more stress you experience.

Once you realize that you only have three choices, you can make decisions sooner and reduce the level of stress. If you're not satisfied with your first choice, you can usually choose again.

Each of these options can have a positive outcome:

1. Accept the situation. This means accepting the situation as it is (not as you wish it were or think you can make it), adopting a positive attitude, and letting go of any resentment or negativity you feel about what is happening. There may still be problems, but you are determined to work through them and do your best to come to an agreement.

2. Leave the situation. Some circumstances are so destructive or unproductive that it's best to leave. Leaving can be a healthy option, but be sure you've considered all

the alternatives before you exit. Don't let initial fears or momentary discomfort keep you from having what you want. Make sure you won't regret your decision later.

3. Change your behavior. Notice that this alternative isn't "change the situation," but "change *how you act in* the situation." You can't always change the circumstances around you, but you can change the way you respond:

- You can self-correct if something you are doing or saying isn't working.
- You can release negative emotions or thoughts instead of holding on to them and letting them set the tone for your interaction.
- You can let go of assumptions you may be making or attitudes you may have adopted.

Sometimes changing how you act in the situation will change what is going on. Sometimes it won't. If you've done your best and the circumstances are still intolerable, at least you can leave with a clear head and a clean conscience.

TECHNIQUE #56:
Don't Let Others Determine Your Behavior or Your Self-Worth

When you put forward your proposal in Step Three, you have to be steering your own course. When obstacles arise, you need to hold that course even more firmly. Don't think less of yourself because others are being difficult, and don't let them prevent you from taking the high road.

If people respond negatively or inappropriately, remember that they may be more upset with themselves than they are with you. By the same token, look to see what is really making you angry before lashing out. In any case, hold to your own standards and *act, don't react.*

Bishop Pierre Dumaine of San Jose once said, "You never have as good a chance to look good as when you are around someone who doesn't." Turning the other cheek isn't just Biblical morality; it's good strategy.

I was once walking down a New York street with Howard Raiffa, whom I consider one of the world's most thoughtful and creative negotiators. Amid all the gleaming skyscrapers, we came upon the old, run-down newsstand where Howard always bought his morning paper. It had a warped plywood counter, peeling green paint, and a dilapidated roof of corrugated metal jutting out at an angle.

Sam, who stood behind the counter, wasn't in much better shape than his newsstand. Howard put some money on the counter and paused in our conversation long enough to say a cheerful, "Good morning, Sam!"

Sam snarled, barked "*Hah!*" and walked to the back of the stand. I jumped; Howard didn't.

I asked Howard, "What do you suppose is the matter?"

Howard smiled and said, "This is actually one of his up days."

"How could you tell?" I asked.

"He had a special lilt in his step."

"How long have you been coming to this newsstand, Howard?"

"About ten years."

I asked Howard why he was so nice to someone who was so unpleasant. He turned to me and said something I'll never forget.

"Why should I let someone else determine my behavior?"

TECHNIQUE #57:
Discover an Admirable Motive, Especially When You Don't Think They Have One

This is often the only way out when obstacles block a negotiation. Everyone has some positive intention or admirable motive, even if it's only to get the issue settled and make it go away.

Your willingness to focus on other people's positive intent

can actually bring their best qualities to the surface. When you speak to their good side, you are more likely to experience it. If you comment on their problems or weaknesses, that is what you encourage.

Matt and Neil's argument over their company's direction had turned into a deadlocked battle of wills. Matt thought Neil was running the place into the ground—thinking only in the short term, pulling out profits for his own personal gain, and leaving nothing on which to build.

He couldn't see an up side to Neil's behavior until he forced himself to look for one. Even then, all he could see was that Neil was trying to provide for his family. It wasn't much, but it gave Matt what he needed to stay connected to Neil. He saw a man fighting to benefit people he loved, and that gave him some grounds to respect Neil and keep the discussion going. They finally reached a compromise, and in this case, it was a triumph even to finish the negotiation.

Discovering other people's admirable motives can be the last thread that keeps you connected and allows you to go forward. The trick is to look for those admirable motives when you least feel like doing so.

TECHNIQUE #58:
Give the Kind of Energy You Want to Get Back, and Pay Attention to the Qualities in Others That You Want to See More

You get back whatever energy you put out to others. If your approach is positive, theirs is more likely to be positive as well. If you are negative, they may also adopt a negative posture.

One way this principle works is that you always see more of whatever qualities in people you praise, criticize, or give any kind of attention. If you focus on people's limitations, they will give you an endless string of limitations. If you focus on what they are doing right, they will give you more of that.

People will always go where the attention is; it doesn't matter whether that attention is positive or negative. You get better results when you praise your salespeople for high sales figures than when you beat them up for not producing. The person who always turns in a late report is not likely to change his or her behavior if it is always spotlighted with comments like, "I hate it when you do this! It ruins my record-keeping and makes me look bad!"

Pay attention to, talk about, and respond to those parts of other people that you want to see more of, even when your inclination is to pay more attention to the negative.

The Fork in the Road

Just as you can encourage certain behaviors by giving them energy, you can sometimes defuse situations by completely withdrawing your energy from them.

Whenever you are in conflict with another person, you stand at a fork in the road. You can confront the problem directly, or you can keep from investing any more energy. This is how the two options work:

1. *Confront the problem directly.* If you think others will respond honestly and you can resolve the issue, confront them directly. Ask them what is going on with them and what they are feeling. Then tell them how you feel, and work through the conflict until you come to a solution.
2. *Do not invest any more energy.* This is not the flight part of fight or flight, or a way to avoid confrontation, but a far more difficult alternative.

Withdrawing your energy completely means that you don't discuss the problem, or how you feel about it, with the other person involved. Instead, you act as if nothing has happened and handle your emotional reactions on your own. You work it through with yourself until *you harbor no resentments*. If you continue to blame the other person, you are still feeding energy to the situation. You have to let it go completely and forever, without expecting anything back.

Next comes the hard part: *You do not then discuss the problem with anyone else.* That would also be giving it energy, and getting yourself even further tangled in it.

Choose this alternative only when you believe that confronting the problem directly would make it worse, when you are convinced that others will—

- Deny that there is a problem,
- Resist dealing with it, or
- Escalate it out of control.

Ivy spent hours each day on the phone complaining to friends about her awful husband, Bert. This infuriated Jessica, who sat at the next desk. She hated Ivy's whining tone, resented her taking so much company time for personal problems, and couldn't stand the way Ivy popped her gum. Jessica had had trouble with Ivy since the day she arrived.

None of Jessica's attempts to handle problems with Ivy had been successful. Ivy had either started screaming a defense or had grabbed her purse and stomped out of the building. Jessica had little reason to believe that Ivy would respond any better to a suggestion that she quit complaining and get back to work. She even suspected that Ivy knew how much the constant whining bothered her and was enjoying her discomfort.

Jessica realized that she was going to have to withdraw her energy completely from the situation. Instead of casting dark glances Ivy's way each time she picked up the phone, Jessica ignored her completely and threw herself into other work.

She spent some time exploring why Ivy's behavior bothered her so much, and realized one reason was that her own marriage wasn't in terrific shape. Hearing Ivy complain about Bert reminded her of her own problems at home.

Instead of joining her coworkers in Ivy-bashing on breaks and at lunch every day, Jessica started taking walks during her coffee breaks and didn't discuss the situation with anyone.

Gradually, over about a month, Ivy's whiny calls became less frequent. She was no longer getting a reaction. Half the fun of raking Bert over the coals was all the attention it got her; it lost a lot of its appeal when she was no longer able to get a rise out of Jessica. Ivy eventually moved on to other problems, but Jessica had stopped being bothered by her as soon as she took matters into her own hands and withdrew her energy from the situation.

You can also use this principle if you are the third party to whom someone is complaining. Suppose Lisa came to you with terrible stories about your best friend, Michael. Your first instinct might be to lash out at her, deny whatever she said, and defend Michael—but instead, you realize that you're at the fork in the road.

You know Lisa couldn't handle a direct confrontation, so you withdraw your energy. You stare back at her. She stares at you. What can you say that won't feed energy to the situation? When in doubt, look to the other person's positive intent. Speak to Lisa as if she has already done the right thing.

"What did Michael say when you told him that?" you could ask, suggesting that she has spoken directly to the person with whom she has the problem.

The worst thing she can say is, "Well, I didn't talk to *him!* He *is* the problem!"

Continue to act as if she means well, and ask, "Do you have any concerns about our relationship?" If she brings up a problem, you have a chance to resolve that issue. If she says, "I have no problem with you," you have no choice but to treat it as the truth. Continue in a neutral or positive vein with "I'm glad. If you ever do have a concern, I hope we can talk about it directly and comfortably."

Don't blame or take sides. Give her a sense of what you want from her in your own relationship. Even when what you want from people is uncomfortable—telling the truth, for instance—they are usually so relieved to have some direction in this area that they do whatever you ask.

You might then return to the subject of Michael—continuing to look to her best intentions and showing support at every turn—and say, "When you talk to Michael, I'd be glad to come with you if you like."

You do not then talk to Michael—or anyone else—about Lisa and what she said. These kinds of talks may make you look like a saint, but you'll be keeping the issue alive and contributing to the climate of backbiting and indirect communication.

You have to choose one of these two alternatives: confronting the other person directly or withdrawing your energy.

The situation only gets more muddled and difficult if you try to straddle the fence. "Sort of" being direct or "sort of" withdrawing brings "sort of" responses from others. You don't know what game you're playing, so you can't win.

TECHNIQUE #59:
Remember That Men and Women Are Different

The battle of the sexes didn't end when women picked up their briefcases and marched off to work; the field just expanded to include the office.

One reason men and women both attract and infuriate one another is that they are so different, and this dynamic doesn't change just because they have contact at an office instead of in a restaurant or a home.

Understanding the basic differences in the way men and women communicate, negotiate, and resolve conflicts is no longer just a social advantage; it is a professional necessity.

Again, the key is to see these differences not as impediments and obstacles, but as opportunities for both men and women to learn from one another and develop their undeveloped sides. Women can teach men to be more sensitive to what is going on around them, for instance, and men can teach women to solve problems more directly.

The differences between how men and women operate in the professional sphere are not unlike their differences in personal areas.

1. *Men want to prioritize; women want to feel and empathize*. As a result, men often think women are unfocused and unproductive, and women think men are insensitive and unfeeling.

Mel went crazy when he found out that his assistant, Amy, had circumvented procedures and gotten the payroll department to give an advance to an employee who was leaving on vacation. To him, it seemed like deliberate insubordination, an intentional violation of the rules and a challenge to his authority. To her, it was a simple act of kindness, a way of helping someone out, and had very little to do with Mel.

Understanding some of the basic differences between men and women might allow Mel and Amy to see one another's perspective more clearly, and even to learn from one another. Amy might come to appreciate the value of procedures more and learn not to take matters into her own hands when the spirit moved her. Mel might learn to be more flexible and understanding.

2. Men want to solve problems; women want to talk about them, although these tendencies are changing as women spend more time in the workplace. Men get impatient when women don't go immediately for solutions; women think men miss many of the important points because they just want to gloss things over and get rid of the problem.

Josh used something he'd learned in his personal life to make things go more smoothly at the office. He and his wife, Nan, had had a fight about where to go on vacation. To make peace and get the issue settled, he had given in and agreed to her choice, Hawaii, but Nan still wasn't happy.

She kept wanting to talk about it more, to know what he felt. Josh found himself getting angry, until he realized that Nan was more interested in the process of their discussion and the nuances of their relationship—how he felt, what he really wanted and why, the dynamic between them before, during, and after this fight—than she was in where they spent their vacation.

She wanted to *talk* with him, not necessarily to win the argument. Understanding what she really wanted allowed him to give it to her without feeling frustrated or cheated.

At the office the next day, his colleague Marcy wanted to go out to lunch and discuss a presentation they were making the next week. He already had a good plan and he knew Marcy was extremely competent in this area, so he thought the lunch would be a waste of time; however, his experience with Nan made him suspect that Marcy needed to talk about what they were going to say and go through this "connecting" process in order to feel comfortable with the presentation.

3. Women notice the subtleties of interactions between people; men tend to be more oblivious in this area. Women are far more likely to pick up on body language, tone of voice, facial expressions, and other nuances than men are. These things are obvious to women, and they can't understand why men are so blind to them. They think men must be totally uninterested not to notice. In fact, the men may be very interested once these issues are called to their attention.

A couple attends a dinner party, and all the way home the woman talks about the obvious attraction between one man and another man's wife, or the tension between a woman and her sister. The man looks at her blankly. He is mystified. She must have been at a completely different party. He saw none of this and can't imagine what she's talking about. She thinks he must have been asleep the whole evening.

4. *Men tend to hold on to their emotions longer; women say what they feel, get it out, let go, and move on.* Men may be slower to initiate emotional discussions or to show their emotions, but once they have allowed these feelings to come out, they need more time to recover their equilibrium than women do. Women think, "This is over, isn't it? We already talked about this. I've gotten through it. You're still sulking. What's the matter with you?"

Gwen and Burke had a fight Saturday night over whether to let their thirteen-year-old son, Jordan, spend the summer with her parents on their Wisconsin farm. Jordan wanted to go and Gwen couldn't understand Burke's reluctance to let him. In the course of their argument, it emerged that Burke had been sent off to a very unpleasant summer with his father's brother when he was about Jordan's age and still harbored a great deal of anger and resentment toward his parents over that issue.

Gwen was glad that he let these emotions surface and that they decided to let Jordan go to Wisconsin, but she couldn't understand why Burke was still edgy and withdrawn all day Sunday. As the week wore on, he gradually returned to his normal, affable self, but Gwen learned a lesson from his behavior. After disagreements or emotional interactions with male colleagues, she let them have a wide berth for a few days and gave them a chance to recover.

5. *Men and women have different body languages.* We looked earlier at women's tendency to "leak" emotion through their hands and to move around more than men. Men leak emo-

tions through their feet, especially when they cross one leg over the other and bounce the crossed foot.

When men leak emotion this way, women instinctively know that something is wrong. They feel uneasy and start talking sooner, faster, and longer—which of course aggravates the situation and makes the men even jumpier. By the time men start this foot-leaking, they are usually too far gone, too emotionally upset, to deal effectively with the situation. Women should let it go for the time being and bring up the subject another time.

Men also do what I call "sidling." When they first meet one another and know that they want to cooperate, not compete, they go out of their way not to make any threatening gestures or strike any confrontive poses. They sidle, standing side by side or at right angles, often with their arms folded, and often swaying back and forth as they talk.

This keeps them from standing face to face, which is the most confrontational posture. They are looking in the same direction and moving together, both of which suggest that they are on the same team. Sidling is a way of saying, "We're not threats to one another. Let's get down to work."

A mother I know used some of these techniques on her young son. She went into his room (his territory, where he would feel most comfortable) and got down on the floor with him, leaning back against the bed and facing the same way he was facing, with their eyes on the same level. Then she said, "Where do you want to put your toys away?" She didn't tell him what to do; rather, she asked his opinion. He offered no resistance at all, and started putting the toys in their chest. We're all children on these nonverbal and subconscious levels.

6. *Men feel bad when they don't solve problems; women feel bad when they're not liked.* Men are less likely to ask for advice or direction because they feel more like failures if they can't solve a problem themselves. Women, on the other hand, are more likely to take criticism personally and to be devastated by what was meant as constructive input.

You can use this information to make more effective proposals in your personal, as well as your professional life.

When proposing action to a man, avoid sounding as if he can't solve the problem:

- "I know we could find the restaurant ourselves, but I'm too tired to deal with the map right now. Would you mind if we just asked someone?"
- "I know you could explain that investment to me, but I hate to take our time together for that. Why don't I just ask my stockbroker Monday morning?"

When proposing action to a woman, watch out for her wariness of not being liked and her tendency to interpret suggestions as personal criticism:

- "You look wonderful in the green dress; I just think the red one would be better for this particular occasion."
- "You handled the situation beautifully; I just want to make doubly sure Billy understands he's to be in by midnight."

When you are aware of how both your sex and the other sex communicate and operate, you can make allowances for these differences and even learn from them.

Again, whatever behaviors you give most attention to will be repeated. If you say to a man, "You have no feelings, you're so insensitive," you're likely to get more of that behavior. If you say, "I so appreciated your telling me how you felt then," you'll get more emotional connection.

A man will get better results with "I appreciate your giving me that new approach to solving our problem" than with "You're such a ditz. When are you going to learn to concentrate and get things done?"

TECHNIQUE #60:
Develop a Semipermeable Membrane

Good negotiators have two apparently contradictory qualities:

1. They can extend beyond themselves and know what others are feeling.
2. They maintain their own space, their own boundaries.

They seem to have semipermeable membranes, like the walls of our bodies' cells. Some fluid passes through these cell walls, but there is a definite distinction between inside the cell and outside.

To propose action in a way others can accept, and to handle obstacles when they arise, you need semipermeable boundaries between yourself and other people. You have to experience some of what they feel in order to sense what's going on and read the situation accurately, but you also have to maintain your own space and be true to your own wants.

Women are taught to have much more permeable boundaries than men. They are inclined to feel everything that others feel and sense exactly what is going on, but they often lose their own boundaries in the process.

Men are more clear about their boundaries but less sensitive to what others are feeling, so they don't always understand the situation as clearly. They can say, "These are my rights; these are your rights"—whether they are married to the person, like the person, hate the person, or have just met the person—but they can't always tell what that person is feeling, or express their own feelings well.

This is another area in which men and women can learn from one another. Judy and Miles spent a week with his mother after his father's death. The mother was a very emotional woman and, naturally, she was grief-stricken. Judy seemed to feel everything she felt, but the more tears Judy shed, the more stoic Miles became. Finally he yelled at her, "Can't you turn it off for one night?" She screamed back, "How can you be so cold? Are you dead inside?"

Judy's boundaries were too permeable; Miles's weren't permeable enough. In an effort not to experience his mother's grief, he repressed his own. Later, after they'd returned home and gotten some distance, Miles and Judy saw how they could learn from one another.

The best negotiators and conflict-resolvers—

- Sense what others feel, but maintain their own space, speaking and proposing action from within their own boundaries.
- Take care of their own needs first so that they can remain sensitive to others, just as flight attendants always warn parents to put on their own oxygen masks first so that they can better help their children.

TECHNIQUE #61:
Contrast the Disadvantages of Quitting with the Benefits of Continuing

When obstacles arise and nothing seems to be working, it's tempting to throw in the towel. The pain and effort of continuing the negotiation can seem overwhelming, and all you want is *out!* In this sense, a negotiation can be like a relationship.

Frustration is natural when things aren't going well, but stop and think before you act. If you stop negotiating and give up, how will you feel tomorrow? Next week? Next year? What is the down side of not reaching an agreement? What do you stand to lose? Will you regret having acted hastily? Take the time to consider the advantages of continuing and the disadvantages of quitting.

Others may also experience frustration and want to quit. If you sense that they want to give up, and you want to continue, stop talking about the issues for a moment and switch to the subject of "continuing versus quitting."

Ask them what they think are the advantages of continuing versus the disadvantages of quitting. Get them to talk about it in their own words if possible. If they seem too overwrought, tired, discouraged, or frustrated to come up with their own ideas, fill in the blanks for them.

You might say something like "I know we're all very tired and our prospects for coming to an agreement don't look too good right now, but if we can stick it out and work through this we'll have something important to show and can be proud of ourselves. If we give up, the situation still won't be resolved and we'll have wasted all this time and effort."

It is almost always better to continue, and one way to clarify this for yourself and others is to contrast—

- The best-case scenario of reaching the agreement versus the worst-case scenario of *not* coming to terms.
- The momentary comfort of leaving versus the discomfort later when you have to live without the agreement.
- The threats posed by continuing versus the opportunities if you negotiate successfully.

TECHNIQUE #62:
Keep the Momentum Going by Reviewing the Progress You've Made So Far

When the discussion gets bogged down, a good way to pick up everybody's energy is to review the progress you've made so far. This focuses attention on the positive things you've already accomplished, and highlights your ability to work through issues.

Instead of letting the energy drop even further or allowing the discussion to wander off course, say:

- "Let's take a two-minute time-out to review what we've already accomplished. We've made decisions about three of the five things we're here to discuss—salaries, benefits, and hours—and we're doing a great job!"
- "I know this is a tough issue, but look what we've already done. We've sailed over the biggest hurdle, deciding the general direction of the campaign, and now we just need to find the best ways to execute that plan."

This technique also works on a personal level. Kim and Bart were in the midst of an amicable divorce and hoping to save attorneys' fees by deciding what they wanted before seeing the lawyers. They got together one night and worked for an hour before every issue started becoming problematic.

Finally Kim said, "Look, let's shift the focus for a minute here. We're getting grouchy now, but look what we've already accomplished. We're clear about the most important thing, the kids and visitation. We've also decided about the money, which is the second biggest thing, and we made a good start on the things in the house before we started getting tired. Let's take a walk around the block for some fresh air and see if we can't finish up tonight."

TECHNIQUE #63:
P-A-C-E Yourself

Whenever difficulties or obstacles arise, look to see whether there is something in your behavior or attitude that you can correct.

You are the element in the negotiation over which you have the most control. If something you are doing, saying, or thinking is the source of the problem, it will be relatively easy to correct.

P-A-C-E yourself to get back on track:

Pinpoint what is happening.
Analyze what needs to happen to improve the situation.
Change your behavior.
Evaluate how this self-correction is working.

Norm, Cynthia, and their two children were spending the evening getting ready for a camping trip the next weekend. The kids were very excited, running around and making a lot of noise, and Norm kept yelling at them to put things back in their proper places and get with the program. Cynthia watched the smiles fade from their faces again and again as Norm got angrier with their antics and more forceful in his determination to get things done. She took their side and told him to lighten up, which only created more tension.

His perspective was that they were there to get the equipment ready, and that everybody else was trying to thwart his efforts. The kids' perspective was that Daddy was a grouch and ruining their fun. Cynthia's perspective was that Norm should understand that the camping trip was about having fun together, and not throw cold water on the kids' excitement.

She knew what she wanted—for the whole family to get their gear together, and also have some fun—and she knew that her siding with the kids against Norm was not producing that result. Cynthia used the P-A-C-E approach to self-correct:

1. She **P**inpointed what was happening. Her resistance to Norm was polarizing the group and making him even more grouchy.

2. She **A**nalyzed what she needed to do to improve the situation and get everybody on the same side. First, she had to get on the same team with Norm.

3. She **C**hanged her behavior. She took Norm aside, put her arms around him, and apologized for taking the kids' side. She reminded him that the whole reason they were going on the trip was to have fun together, and pointed out that the kids' enthusiasm was fading because he was treating it as a job instead of as family time. She let him know that she was on his side and wanted the two of them to be the nucleus of fun around which the family gathered. When they got back to the living room, Norm was her focus. She supported him, smiled at him, and made him the leader of their team.

4. She **E**valuated how this self-correction was working. Norm was smiling, the kids were having a great time again, and Cynthia realized that she was having much more fun as well.

TECHNIQUE #64:
At Each Step, Give People a Stake in the Outcome

People can lose interest and stop negotiating in earnest when—

- They don't think they can have what they want.
- They think they're only representing their huge and impersonal company.
- They don't feel that they are part of the team.

They may appear sullen, unresponsive, or bored, but the results are the same—the talks bog down and you have trouble getting your agreement. Unless you get them involved, these people can sabotage the whole negotiation.

The best way to get them involved is to give them a stake in the outcome. Let them know they can have some of what they want, that you plan to make sure the powers that be in their company know they did a good job, and that their input is wanted and needed. Do whatever it takes to bring them to life and get their minds as well as their bodies into the room.

Some other ways to encourage their participation are:

- Invite their opinion.
- Ask them to do some of the "committee work" or research.
- Get their responses to others' suggestions.
- Seat them in the middle of the group; don't let them hang out on the edges.

People who are active participants reach agreements more quickly and are more satisfied with the results.

TECHNIQUE #65:
Point Out That No Situation Has to Be Win/Lose

This reaffirms your good faith and your intention to find a solution that works for everyone. Saying out loud that you can all come away as winners is a way to reestablish your connection and remind everyone why the negotiation got started in the first place.

You can turn the energy around simply by saying, "You know, this doesn't have to be a win/lose proposition." This is a direct, specific statement that you're not out to get the other person and that you'd like to be more connected. It is an offer to be on the same team and to try to work things out together, a peace offering that you can make without giving up anything.

Again, these techniques apply to obstacles you encounter at home as well as at work. Elaine and Carter both had hectic careers and looked forward to Sunday as the day they spent together, completely away from work. One Sunday Elaine woke up full of energy; she wanted to take a run, then bike to the country for a picnic. Carter felt he'd overdone it the minute he opened his eyes; the most he could consider doing was sliding out of bed for a sumptuous brunch, then slinking home to the couch for a day of shameless food consumption and TV sports-watching.

"But you're wasting the *whole day*," Elaine screamed in frustration.

"Get off my back," he returned. "One day a week I can do what I want, and this is it. I run around all week!"

"So do I, but not in the fresh air! It's a beautiful day! Come on, let's go."

The argument escalated until eleven o'clock rolled around; they were both having a terrible day. Carter was the first to realize what was happening and said, "Hey, let's not blow the whole Sunday. This doesn't have to be win/lose; let's figure something out so we can both have a good day off."

Carter and Elaine weren't stupid people, but they were human. They knew that no situation has to be win/lose, but they had to be reminded. By doing the reminding, Carter put them back on the same team. They compromised on a ride (in the car) to the country, where Elaine took a run and Carter took a nap before their picnic.

TECHNIQUE #66:
Be Courteous and Preserve Mutual Respect, Especially When You Least Feel Like It

When others don't cooperate, your best response is to cooperate more. Being courteous can't hurt any situation, and being discourteous can't help. The time to be most courteous is when you least feel like it.

Find something to like or respect about the other person, and speak to that issue. If you can't find anything to like or respect, be courteous simply to honor yourself and the kind of climate for communication you want to create.

One of the benefits of being courteous is that it keeps you from appearing threatening. You can't always anticipate what others will find threatening from day to day, or situation to situation; the courteous approach gives you general protection.

My client Kenneth tells a story that shows how unpredictable our perceptions of what is threatening can be. His Montreal manufacturing business experienced an extremely tense and difficult time several years ago when board members and top executives disagreed about corporate direction and, at the height of the turmoil, many of the employees walked out on strike.

Kenneth's assistant, Margaret, was his mainstay during this time. She was cool, calm, collected, and imperturbable in the face of flaring tempers, executives yelling up and down the halls, contradictory orders to her and those around her, even having her tires slashed in the parking lot. At one point, an irate secretary threw a fat record book past Margaret at her demanding supervisor. Margaret was on the phone with someone threatening Kenneth's life at the time, but caught the record book in midair while calmly suggesting that the man call back when Kenneth was in.

One morning after disagreements subsided, the strike was settled, and life at the company was returning to normal, Kenneth heard a bloodcurdling cry from the direction of Margaret's desk. She ran into his office, screaming hysterically and completely undone. A small bird had flown into her window and was darting around the reception area. Margaret didn't stop screaming until he managed to herd it back out the window by flapping his arms.

You never know what's going to upset people, so it's best not to do anything that might be interpreted as threatening.

Part of courtesy is preserving mutual respect. Never embarrass or humiliate others, regardless of how upset you get.

Safeguard the relationship—even if, at the moment, you never want to see the other person again. You will either gain an ally, or avoid making an enemy who might come back to haunt you later.

Leave the other person room to save face and to self-correct. If his or her figures don't add up, it's not necessary to say, "You added wrong. See? Two and two is four!" To preserve respect, you might say something like "I'm not sure how that adds up. Could you go over it again?" Let the other person make the correction, rather than doing it yourself.

Charlotte was talking to her new boss, Drew, about her upcoming presentation. She had written everything out and sent him a copy a week in advance, but when they sat down, she saw that he didn't have his copy. He rummaged around in his files, in his mail, in several piles of paper around his desk, and was obviously embarrassed that he'd misplaced it.

Instead of getting angry or defensive and blurting, "Did you lose your copy? Did you even *read* it?" Charlotte found a way for him to save face. "Oh, I'm sorry, Drew," she said. "I forgot to make the copy I was going to bring you. Let me step out a minute and do that." It was a small thing, but it set the tone for their meeting, which went very well for Charlotte.

Being right is no help when it comes to staying connected to others or getting the agreement. It is far more valuable to be known as someone who is respectful and courteous, and who can be trusted to act in the mutual best interest.

In the heat of an argument, it's easy to forget how important it is to preserve relationships. Chances are, you'll be negotiating with these people again. Even if you don't, you'll feel better about yourself and the situation if you preserve mutual respect—especially when you appear to have the upper hand or to be the winner.

Obstacles are a part of life, and part of any negotiation or conflict resolution. As you meet challenges along the way, use these techniques to get past the stumbling blocks, find new strengths and skills, and bring forth the best in yourself.

EXERCISES

1. The last time you ran into obstacles, which of the techniques in this chapter did you use?
2. Which others might have been helpful? How could you have applied those techniques to get the negotiation back on track?

OVERCOME OBSTACLES II: What to Do When Your Nightmares Come True

> You must be the foremost expert on you. If the other party recognizes your hot buttons and triggers better than you do, they become the pilot of the process.
>
> —GEORGE ATHOS

In the last chapter, we discussed general principles for handling "people problems." This chapter is about pinpointing the specific types of people who are most difficult for you—those who seem to hold remote controls aimed at your hot buttons—and learning to manage your encounters with them.

The people who will present the biggest obstacles for you, and who will present them most frequently, are likely to be either—

1. Those whom you see regularly at home or work and for whom you have strong feelings—good or bad.
2. The particular "types" of people who push your specific hot buttons and can catch you by surprise to sabotage a negotiation.

TECHNIQUE #67:
Identify the People Who Bother You Most and Learn to Manage Your Encounters with Them

Each of us has our own unique set of triggers and our own set of "difficult people." The individual who makes Person A nuts may have no effect at all on Person B. Another individual may infuriate Person B, but go entirely unnoticed by Person A.

When you can pinpoint which types of people irritate you most, you can work to defuse that specific set of hot buttons so that you're no longer bothered by those people.

In the meantime, plan ahead for your encounters with them so that you aren't caught off guard. Here are strategies for dealing with six types of people who are often found at the center of conflict:

1. Dominators
2. Know-it-alls
3. Agreeables
4. "Won't work" people
5. Bumps on a log
6. Complainers

Dominators

These are the aggressive people who try to take over every meeting and impose their will on the group. They are the classic Kings of the Mountain.

Use these techniques to keep them from dominating the negotiation:

1. Don't escalate the conflict by becoming as aggressive as they are, "standing up to them," or confronting them directly.

2. Don't resist them, but don't withdraw. Stay calm in the face of their offensive behavior, but don't run away. If you give in to fight or flight, they have won.

3. Mirror their body language and tone of voice, but be careful that you don't appear to confront them. When you have matched their level of intensity, gradually decrease your own volume. They will unconsciously follow you into "cooler" body language, verbal tone, and behavior.

4. Focus on your own goals, not their behavior, and keep moving toward a solution. Remember, you will get more of whatever behavior and qualities you give attention to.

5. Acknowledge their concerns. You don't have to agree with them, but let them know that you've heard what they said. If you don't, they will just keep repeating themselves.

6. Allow them to let off steam. Sometimes they will simply run down of their own accord.

7. Let them save face. Act as if they did not intend to grab all the power. If you expect the best, you may at least get "better."

8. Avoid blaming them or using emotion-laden words that might heat them up again.

9. Make clear to them the conditions under which you will and will not communicate with them in the future. For instance, you may not want to talk with them again unless they agree not to interrupt when you are speaking. Or you may insist on having a third party present. Make the consequences reflect what is important to them.

You might say, "John, I want us to work something out and I sense that you do, too, but I can't operate in an environment where I'm constantly interrupted. We're going to have to start a 'no interrupting' ground rule or I won't be able to continue."

Know-It-Alls

These are the people with the answer to everything. They thrive on the game of one-upmanship, and always have to be the smartest or the best.

1. Acknowledge their accomplishments. Sometimes this is all they really want. If you do it up front, they don't have to beg for it throughout the meeting.

2. Recognize similar accomplishments in others who are present to spread attention throughout the group. ("Congratulations to Jerry for landing the Thompson account . . . and to Ellen for bringing in Crocker.")

3. "Bridge" from what they say to issues that involve and interest all the members of the group. ("Because of Jerry's great job with the Thompson account, we'll need to gear up and hire a few more people. Any suggestions?")

4. Acknowledge them, then turn to ask someone else's opinion. ("Thanks, Jerry. Evelyn, do you have any ideas for the Thompson account?")

Agreeables

They are anxious to please, but often don't keep their commitments. They tend to have low self-esteem and fear rejection, conflict, and criticism.

1. Be specific in your expectations. Give them detailed directions, and don't leave much to chance or initiative. Tell them exactly what you want. ("Eric, can you have that written up and make ten copies before our four o'clock meeting?" "Susan, I need to be on a flight to Los Angeles before five o'clock today. If one airline can't schedule it, keep calling until you find a flight. If you haven't found one by noon, let me know.")

2. Find out whether they understand what you have said. Ask them whether you are being clear, and whether they have any questions.

3. Solicit their ideas. Find out whether they see a better way of doing things. Ask whether there are any alternatives they would prefer. Don't count on them to tell you these things without being asked, even if they have a brilliant solution.

4. Tie the solution to their value system, self-image, and relationships. This gives them a stake in the outcome and the promise of validation. Get them more actively involved wherever possible. Make sure they see your agreement as something for which they can win approval.

5. Ask them how they want the follow-up to proceed. You will always have to follow them up, and it's easier to do so if they've participated in the follow-up plan.

6. Get witnesses. The greater the number of people who know about the commitment, the greater the likelihood that they will keep it.

"Won't Work" People

Their first comment will be "It won't work" or "We've tried this before" or "Everyone knows this will fail." They reject others' ideas. If you say "black," they say "white." These combative people don't know the meaning of the word "teamwork." They exude negativity and seem determined to blow even the smoothest negotiations out of the water.

1. *Minimize their contact with the rest of the group.* Don't let them be the bad apples that spoil the bushel.

2. *Reduce their responsibilities, if possible.* If whatever they touch turns to dust, don't let them touch anything important.

3. *Define penalties for specific negative behaviors*: interrupting, criticizing, etc. Otherwise, they can do these things with impunity, and the rest of the group has no way to stop them.

4. *Don't waste energy venting your frustration with them*—either directly or to the rest of the team. That only feeds them power. Rather, shift your attention to other team members. Instead of blaming the "no" people, compliment the others.

5. *Have the team establish specific guidelines for communicating and working together*, so that they can use these agreements to maintain a healthy work environment, even in the face of the "no" people's negativity.

Bumps on a Log

These are the people you have to light a fire under to get even minimal participation. They may not care what happens, or they may have found that the minimal course of action is always the safest. The less they do, the safer they are.

1. *Ask them directly what their expectations are* for the negotiation and be clear about yours. This gets them involved from the start and forces them to define their needs publicly.

2. *Mirror their behavior.* Don't over-talk. Be silent when they are silent; wait them out. Then gradually become more animated, bringing up their intensity along with yours. Be careful not to go too fast and pass them by, or they will sink into a trance again.

3. *As a last resort, force their participation by giving them a choice*

between two alternative solutions—neither of which is "Take no action."

Complainers

They criticize and complain constantly, either directly or by whining. Nothing is ever right, and they let you know it. Unlike the "won't work" people, who knock down others' ideas, they knock anything, even unasked.

1. Listen to them and hear their complaints. Sometimes people keep repeating themselves because they don't think they've been heard.

2. Acknowledge that you heard what they said. Go over the situation with them in factual, nonemotional language. Take the charge off what they say by showing them the bare facts of the matter, uncolored by their negative feelings.

3. Ask what solutions they would advocate and corner them into moving from complaining to creating part of a positive plan.

4. If they complain to you about someone else, tell them to communicate directly with that person. Send them back to the person with whom they have the problem and tell them to discuss it only with someone who can do something about it. Don't let them use you as a dumping ground or "complaining post" for their difficulties with others.

5. Determine the point at which you no longer want them around. Figure out how much you can take, under what circumstances, and set your limits. Then tell them where those limits are. They will either shape up or be warned that they won't stay around if they cross that line.

TECHNIQUE #68:
Find Out Why They Upset You and Disarm That Mechanism

Once you have identified the people who upset you most and learned to manage your encounters with them, you can begin to explore *why* they upset you. When you know that, you can disrupt those old patterns so that they no longer have any power over you.

These ten questions help reveal the inner workings of any difficult relationship, whether personal or professional. Try answering them for the three most difficult people in your life.

1. Which of this person's behaviors upset me most?
2. What is my response to these behaviors? What do I feel? What do I do? Do I withdraw or escalate the conflict?
3. When I react to this person's upsetting behaviors, how does the conflict escalate or get swept under the carpet?
4. What unresolved internal issues, childhood experiences, or unacceptable part of myself do this person's behaviors remind me of? Do they trigger any childhood memories? Do the feelings they elicit remind me of any earlier feelings?
5. What do I honestly want out of my interaction with this person?
6. What do I believe this person wants from the interaction?
7. What do I actually get from my relationship with this person?
8. What are the areas of this relationship that I can control?
9. What are the areas of this relationship that I cannot control?
10. How do I want to proceed? Do I want to continue the relationship? If so, what can I do to make it work better for me? Do boundaries or ground rules need to be set? What will I do if the other person doesn't agree to them? Can I let go of this relationship if it proves more destructive than productive or nurturing? Where do I go from here?

These ten questions helped Adam and Jeannine come to terms with a problem that had been fermenting slowly over the eight years of their marriage. Jeannine was the one who answered the questions, and her responses steered the marriage out of serious trouble.

Her main problem was Adam's tendency to withdraw and not share his thoughts or feelings with her. It had gotten to the point that she hardly thought she knew him anymore, and felt almost completely excluded from his life.

Before she could begin answering the ten questions, she had to make sure she framed the issue as *her problem*, and not as *what was wrong with Adam*. She had to ask, "What is it about this situation that triggers me so strongly?" and not "Why is he such a jerk and what can I do to fix him?"

These were her responses:

1. The behavior that upsets me most is when he clams up and won't tell me what he's thinking or feeling. I don't know if it's something from work, or me, or if he's just not happy with anything in his life.

2. The way I respond is to nag him and pester him to talk to me. I feel angry and panicky, and try to force him to communicate.

3. The more I nag, the more he withdraws. Sometimes he even leaves the house. Then I get angry, and pull back from him when he gets home.

4. My unresolved issue is that this is just the way my father acted, except that my mother didn't force him to talk to her and he ended up leaving us for good. I know it doesn't work to nag Adam, but I'm afraid to stop because my mother didn't nag and my dad left. I can't just let him be. If he doesn't talk to me, he'll leave.

5. What I want out of this situation is for me to stop nagging and Adam to start talking to me.

6. I know he wants me to stop nagging, and he may even want to communicate. If he doesn't want to communicate, I need to know that.

7. What I actually get in the relationship is a lot of aggravation and no sharing. I don't feel like I'm even married to him anymore.

8. The areas of the relationship I can control are:

- The level of my nagging.
- The circumstances under which I will stay with him.

9. The areas of the relationship I cannot control are:

- His level of sharing.
- His willingness to be in the relationship under the conditions that I lay down (more sharing).

10. This is how I want to proceed. I want to talk to Adam about how serious the problem is for me and tell him I understand that part of it is my fault for nagging. I want to stop nagging, and I want us to get some counseling. I want to find out if he really wants to communicate with me and I'm just making it hard for him by nagging, or whether he really doesn't want to share with me what he's thinking and feeling.

   If he honestly doesn't want to share his life with me, I want to leave the relationship. If he's willing to try opening up more if I lay off him, and to continue counseling for at least six months, then I'm committed to staying with him. I want to tell him all this tonight.

TECHNIQUE #69:
Tell the People You See Regularly What You Will and Will Not Tolerate

This is another area where you have to take care of your own needs and set boundaries that work for you. You have a right to be different from other people, and to have your own feelings. You have a right to disagree and to set limits on how you want to interact with them.

The important thing is to define specifically what those limits are—what you will tolerate and what you will not—and then—

- Communicate them clearly to other people.

- Stick to what you say. (If you waffle, they won't believe you next time and you'll start playing an entirely different game—one with no rules at all.)

After Jeannine answered the ten questions in the last section, she had to tell Adam clearly and directly what she had discovered about herself and what she wanted from him. She couldn't say, "I think we should go to couples counseling." She had to say, "I've looked carefully at what I need to stay in this relationship, Adam, and one thing is to start couples counseling within three weeks."

She had to let him know how strong her feelings were, and what the consequences would be if he didn't go to counseling.

This isn't about punishing or controlling others, and you must be careful not to use it that way. It's about protecting yourself, letting others know clearly what your boundaries are, and giving them the information they need to support you.

TECHNIQUE #70:
Act, Don't React, When Meeting New People Who Trigger Negative Feelings

No matter how well you master interactions with the people in your life who upset you, you will always be faced with new challenges. No sooner will you feel at ease with one of the old "difficult people" than you will meet a new one. Now you have the tools and techniques to cope with these surprise encounters.

Here are some guidelines for dealing with those new people at the point of contact, when you first realize that the situation is going to be problematic:

1. Don't react immediately. Recognize that they've triggered an emotional response, and that you can't act the way you want to act right now. Don't jump in with your initial emotional reaction. Wait until you've calmed down.

2. *Assess the situation*. What really happened? Whose hot buttons got pushed, and why?

3. *Define the result you want*. Figure out the least you will accept from the situation, the optimum result, and what you would consider a successful resolution.

4. *Plan a strategic response*. Think ahead to what you'll do next and why. Lay out an escape route for "giving up" and withdrawing if nothing works.

5. *Carry out your plan*.

6. *Debrief yourself afterward*. What worked and what didn't work? What did you learn about yourself that will help you in the future? What did you learn about them? How could you do better next time?

TECHNIQUE #71:
Let Go of the Vibrating Pole

When we're around people who are difficult, it's easy to get caught up in our negative emotions—anger, fear, hurt, or resentment. This is like holding on tightly to a vibrating pole. We vibrate and lose focus. The vibrating pole's energy feeds on itself; the more tightly we hold on, the more we react, rather than choosing how we do.

The solution, obviously, is to let go—but how do you do that? In the end, you just have to do it, but here are some suggestions that make it easier:

1. *Go back to Step One and focus on your bottom line* to shift from emotions to issues.

2. *Don't take it personally*. People aren't necessarily out to get you; they're just afraid of not getting what they want.

3. *Remember that getting the result is more important than being right or indulging in negative emotional reactions*.

It's not always easy to pull yourself out of an emotional quagmire, especially when others show no inclination to do so. It takes courage and will, but it's the only way to get what you want.

TECHNIQUE #72:
Use the Ten-Minute Rule

When an argument lasts for more than ten minutes, ask yourself, "Are we arguing about what we think we are, or is a deeper issue not being discussed?"

Then take a ten-minute break to think about that and let tempers cool. When an unacknowledged issue, a power play, resentment, hurt, or fear is lurking behind the issues you're discussing, it can keep you from resolving the issue that's on the table.

If you suspect that you're not talking about the real problem, find a way to bring the hidden issue to the surface. You might say, "George, I wonder if maybe we're talking about the wrong thing here . . ." or "I may have been taking the wrong tack. Maybe we should really be talking about (the real issue) . . . What do you think?"

TECHNIQUE #73:
Stop the Chain Reaction

When the discussion heats up along unproductive lines and starts to spin out of control, take a sharply different tack. Do anything that stops the momentum, changes the energy, and keeps the argument from continuing along its former lines:

- Change the subject.
- Bring someone new into the discussion.
- Shift your location.
- Take a break.

This solution works better in the short term than the long term, but sometimes that's all you need. Once the chain reaction of negative energy has been broken up, you can refocus the discussion in a more positive direction.

TECHNIQUE #74:
Use the Jimmy Swaggart Approach

Televangelist Jimmy Swaggart knew and used a powerful technique for dealing with adversity: *When you're wrong, admit it*. And admit it first, before others say it.

Scandals erupted in Swaggart's and in Jim Bakker's television ministries at about the same time, but the two men took sharply different approaches to their difficulties.

Jim Bakker denied everything, insisting that he'd never done anything wrong and defending himself with every ounce of energy he had. Almost nobody believed him. He never recovered his credibility or the public's respect.

Jimmy Swaggart, on the other hand, tearfully confessed all his wrongdoings on television to millions of people. His style may have been somewhat melodramatic for some tastes, but what he did worked. He never lost his credibility. People may not have liked what he did, but they still believed what he said and many admired the humility it took to confess his "sins" on the air.

If you do something wrong, admitting it openly is both the high moral ground and the best strategy. Deny it, and it will follow you everywhere. Even if what you did was unintentional, use these four steps to make sure the mistake goes away completely and forever:

1. Admit that you were wrong to the person to whom you least want to admit it.
2. Apologize to all the people who were affected, including the people who may not have your best interest at heart.
3. Then repeat your apology and elaborate on it.
4. Explain what you will do differently to correct the mistake, make amends, and keep the problem from recurring.

This approach may be uncomfortable, but it is the only way to make sure that the mistake doesn't stick to you. The added benefit is that your relationships with the people involved often become stronger. They have watched you do something difficult, and are bound to respect that.

TECHNIQUE #75:
"Fog" to Avoid or Postpone a Response

Occasionally, the best strategy for overcoming obstacles is to acknowledge them, yet give no opinion. This kind of "fogging" is a way to postpone or avoid a response.

To fog the issue, acknowledge what they say without either agreeing or disagreeing: "You may have a point" or "That could be true."

Murray had to decide which of his employees would be promoted to a new position created in his department, and he was appalled when Bev burst into his office one afternoon. She had heard that both she and Nadine were being considered and wanted Murray to know in no uncertain terms that she was far better qualified than Nadine.

She went on and on about her qualifications, practically demanding that Murray promise her the position. He wasn't about to be railroaded or even to discuss his thinking with her, but he didn't want to be rude or to start the office rumor mill churning again.

On those rare occasions when Bev left a blank space in the conversation, he "fogged" with phrases like "Yes, you do very well at your present job," "I'll consider that," and "I see."

Thus, he neither agreed nor disagreed, yet she felt heard. She wound down after his continued calm and brief comments and eventually excused herself.

TECHNIQUE #76:
Use the Messy Desk Solution

Some people sideswipe you by pretending to be joking when they make nasty comments. You know they're taking potshots, but they act like friendly kidders. What they say may be true,

yet so trivial that you would feel foolish confronting them—
and even if you did, they would probably say, "Can't you take
a joke?"

They may saunter by, for instance, and chuckle, "My, but
you have a messy desk." To disarm these covert kidders try
the following:

1. Don't disagree or counterattack, which might be your
   instinctive response.
2. Minimize the physical distance between you. Move a step
   closer if possible.
3. Act as if they meant well. Smile and play along with the
   "joke."
4. Acknowledge what they said in nonemotional language
   and tone.

With a "messy desker," for instance, you might stand up,
take a step toward him or her, smile, and say, "You're right,
it certainly is messy." This disarms the messy desker, defuses
what he or she said, keeps you centered, and prevents your
critic from getting what he or she wanted, which was to upset
you.

You can also defuse the situation by laughing with the messy
desker. If he or she says, "My, but you have a messy desk. Is
it art in progress?" you might stand up immediately, grin at
the desk, and agree, "Looks like it, doesn't it?" By reacting
this way, you turn the situation around and make a connection
without compromising your position or self-esteem.

TECHNIQUE #77:
Shift the Spotlight

When someone hogs all the energy and attention and won't
give others a chance to participate—

1. Wait for a pause.
2. Acknowledge the person's comments.
3. Then physically and verbally turn to someone else and

ask his or her view. (Now the hog has two people whom he must interrupt.)

Here is how it works: You lean forward and look at the hog, saying, "That's an interesting perspective." Then you turn to another person and ask, "What have you found?"

When you master negotiating with the people who upset you most, you can reach agreements with almost anyone.

EXERCISES

1. Make a list of the five people in your life whom you find most difficult.
2. Go back and answer the questions in this chapter with each of these five people in mind.

EMPOWER, DON'T COERCE

16

Power resides not in aggressiveness, but in conscious choice.

—STEPHANIE RHEA

True power comes from knowing what you want and being confident that you can get it, from honoring yourself and other people, and from communicating these attitudes effectively.

Power plays a role in every relationship or interaction—whether or not we choose to acknowledge it—and Step Three has a way of bringing hidden issues about power to the surface.

Wielding power with grace and generosity is crucial to Step Three. Proposing action in a way others can accept often means proposing action in a way that makes them feel stronger and better about themselves.

TECHNIQUE #78:
Empower Others, Don't Coerce or Manipulate Them

The healthiest and most productive negotiations are those in which people's power is perceived as being more or less equal. Even when the balance of power is inherently unequal—when one person is the boss and another is the employee, for example—both parties are better off when power is *perceived* as equal.

Using Triangle Talk techniques almost always puts you in the more powerful position. That power can be used positively to empower others, or abused to coerce them into doing your will.

Coercion

Coercive power is manipulative and only effective in the short term. You force or trick people into doing what you want them to do, with no concern for—

- How they feel.
- How long the agreement will work.
- How your relationship will feel after the negotiation.

These coerced agreements rarely last, don't bring much satisfaction to anyone, and usually damage relationships.

Coercive power works from the top down. You have to be on top, and stay on top, in order to use it—and when you're on top, someone is always nipping at your heels. When you start coercing, you have to *keep* coercing or the whole house of cards tumbles.

Coercive power also creates dependency. Good people don't stay around because they can't relax, grow, or flourish in this environment. They aren't allowed to think or do for themselves, and must always turn to the boss for answers and direction. They don't develop their own talents or skills, and it's only a matter of time before they either fade away or counterattack.

Empowering Others

The proof of power is that you can give it away. True power isn't about mowing people down; it's about making choices, getting what you want, feeling good about how you've acted, and enriching relationships.

When you share power—

1. Agreements last longer and work better.
2. People feel better about themselves, one another, and the negotiation. They all have a stake in the outcome, take pride in the agreement, and are committed to making it work. They emerge stronger than they were when they began talking.
3. Relationships are enhanced, not destroyed.

When you are confident about your own power and genuinely want others to win, they automatically feel empowered. Your strength spreads to those around you, just as fear does.

These are some specific techniques you can use to empower others:

1. Make sure you really do want to empower them; don't just pretend to do so because it's a good management technique.
2. Don't fake it. There is no better way to flaunt power than to try to appear equal when dealing with those whom you secretly consider powerless. Remember that everyone has special skills and something unique to contribute.
3. Trust that your respect for others will be communicated nonverbally if it is genuine and heartfelt.
4. Remember that no one can really empower or disempower another person. You are simply bringing the other person's inherent power to the surface and allowing it to work.
5. Focus on what is going well. Acknowledge the positive things that are getting done.
6. Do nothing for others that they can do for themselves, and avoid giving advice. Let them use their own strengths.
7. Be clear yourself. Clarity is the source of your power, and you can't give it away unless you have it.

8. Avoid protecting people from your power. They are strong enough to protect themselves.
9. Provide empathy, not sympathy. Let others know that you understand when things are difficult, but don't pity them or treat them as "poor things."
10. Remember that power comes not from aggressiveness or assertiveness, but from conscious choice.

TECHNIQUE #79:
Pinpoint Your Specific Power Sources

Knowing the sources of your own individual power can help you use it more efficiently, wisely, and effectively.

Power can be either *positional* or *personal*.

Positional power comes from your title or role: father, president, general, boss, etc.

Personal power comes from such intangibles as how you present yourself, how hard you are willing to work, how much information you have, and how much others instinctively want to do things with you and for you.

Use this checklist to discover your particular strengths.

Your Power Checklist

These are the primary sources of personal and positional power:

- Preparation. Whoever has taken the time to do Step One (Know exactly what you want) and Step Two (Find out what they want and make them feel heard) is likely to have more power in any negotiation.
- Legitimacy. Your position or title may carry a certain level of power, but this authority must be backed up by the ability to perform and lead.
- Commitment. Whoever wants the result more is likely to have more power in any given situation.

- Need. The person who has the least need for the relationship or situation always has the most power in it.
- Hard work. Whoever can and will work hardest for the result is most likely to get it.
- Knowledge. This means either having the most information on the subject, or being perceived as the expert.
- Language. If you define the issues more clearly and vividly than others, and speak of them in terms of their value to others, you have the power to (1) choose *which* issues are discussed, and (2) control *how* they are discussed and decided.
- Time. This means not only using your time well, but doing your homework and coming to the negotiation fully prepared.
- Rules and precedent. How was it done before? It will most likely be done that way again.
- Team acquisition and leadership. Whoever can assemble the most able team and inspire their loyalty has the advantage.
- Status and charisma. It may not be fair that those who can attract and charm are in a stronger position, with their own team and with other parties, but it's true.
- Presentation. People in power speak slowly and don't "gush." They are quick to recognize and publicly acknowledge good work or virtue in others. They avoid confrontation and take the slower and more certain, if more circuitous, route.
- Substance and depth. Powerful people's projects, programs, and ideas are backed by "larger than life" visions of lasting importance. This higher purpose inspires people and gives the programs a deeper meaning.

TECHNIQUE #80:
Avoid Power Plays

Nothing reveals weakness more quickly than attempting a power play. Whether or not such power plays "work," people who attempt them have shown that they don't feel secure enough to share power and that they don't respect or honor the other people involved.

These are some coercive power plays that crop up frequently in negotiations:

- "Now, let's be fair." (By my rules.)
- "Can you prove that?" (I know you can't, but it will be fun watching you try.)
- "Be specific. Give me an example." (So I can shoot it down and prove you wrong about everything.)
- "But you just said . . . and now you're saying . . ." (You're being illogical. Don't you know what you mean?)
- "What you really mean is . . ." (I know better than you do what you mean, so listen to me.)
- "Where did you get that idea?" (Don't you know anything? Haven't you done your homework?)
- "What I think you meant was . . ." (We know you're stupid, but I'll be a saint and help you out.)
- "I'll get to that later." (Shut up and let me handle this.)

TECHNIQUE #81:
Take the Power You Need

Most people underestimate their own power and assume they have a weaker position than they actually do. They mistakenly believe that power comes from looking good, from being aggressive, or from knowing a lot. These things may help, but they are not primary sources of power.

These five basic steps are the key to claiming your power in any situation:

1. Identify what you really want and what others really want.
2. When you've decided that you want something, look at the bigger picture. What is your "larger than life" vision,

your deeper purpose? What is the real driving force behind your wanting that particular thing?

3. Rank your wants in order of importance.
4. Determine who controls what you want, and who or what stands in the way of your getting it.
5. Identify the resources that you control, and the people who want those resources.

My client Craig felt out of control when we first met and used these five steps to reclaim his power.

Craig was an attorney at a Seattle law firm who had just turned forty and started to think about his future. He made $55,000 a year; he did his work but didn't bring in many new clients and wasn't on the partnership track. Several younger people made more money and enjoyed more prestige in the firm. The older partners seemed to be ignoring him. On bad days, Craig even thought they might be talking about him. Sometimes he didn't want to get out of bed in the morning.

His wife, Hallie, worked part-time as a bookkeeper, but only brought home about $15,000 a year. His three sons were eleven, thirteen, and fourteen. The family still lived in their "starter" home, which seemed to grow smaller as the boys grew larger.

Craig didn't feel very good about himself, and had begun to realize that unless he started making substantially more money, they couldn't help the boys with college. He knew he had to make some changes, and I suggested he use the five "power steps" as guidelines.

First, Craig identified what he wanted and what others wanted. He wanted to get back on the partnership track at the firm and to feel good about himself. He wanted to be on the way up again, someone who jumped out of bed every morning because he had definite goals and was enthusiastic about the way he was pursuing them.

He shared this vision with his family and warned them that he might have less time to spend with them. He might have to work Saturdays instead of going to the boys' ball games. He and Hallie wouldn't have as much time together or be able to go out as much.

When he asked for their reactions, his youngest son had

some hesitation, but they all realized that this was important to him and were glad to see him excited again.

Second, Craig looked at his larger vision. He didn't want to be a partner just to be a partner. He wanted it because it would bring him and his family financial peace of mind and because it would give him a sense of accomplishment. He would feel as if he had used his gifts and his intelligence well and had done something positive with his life by serving his family and his clients.

Third, he ranked his wants in order of importance and came up with this list:

1. Make partner within three years.
2. Raise my earnings by at least $10,000 a year for the next five years, then reevaluate.
3. Buy a new house within two years.

Fourth, he looked at who controlled what he wanted and who or what stood in the way. The present partners controlled his ability to become a partner, so he scheduled a meeting with them to tell them his intentions, get their advice on how best to proceed, and ask for their support as he pursued his goals.

He knew that the only thing that might stand in his way was his own lack of resolve, and made a deal with Hallie that she would become his coach if he felt his determination flagging.

Fifth, he identified the resources that he controlled and the people who wanted those resources. He had a talent for the law and a gift for litigation. He was diligent when he was motivated and could be assertive enough to bring in new clients if he made that a goal. The people who wanted those talents were the present partners.

Even before he started to realize his goals, Craig felt 100 percent more powerful. He was back in control of his life and in charge of his own destiny. He had started calling the shots again.

He achieved his goals within three years, but even more important, he gained a powerful tool that he could use in any situation to accomplish what he wanted. He knew the power of those five steps and used them over and over again as his challenges got bigger and the stakes got higher.

Keep your eye on the undercurrents of power as you work through Step Three and propose action in a way they can accept. Remember that you don't have to be loud or aggressive to be powerful; you just have to stay focused on what you want and what they want, and honor everyone's right to have it.

EXERCISES

1. When was the last time you were involved in a power struggle? Did the other person try to coerce or manipulate you? Did you try to coerce or manipulate the other person? What was the result?
2. How could you, or the other person, have managed that situation better?

MAKE THEM AN OFFER: Ten Strategies

People take action in order to satisfy essential human needs.

—ABRAHAM MASLOW

You've come up with a proposal that you think is fair to both parties. You've shaped your offer so that others see it in the best light. You've spoken first to their needs and worked through whatever obstacles or power issues have surfaced in the discussion.

Now it's time to make a firm offer. This chapter is about presenting that offer so that it has the best chance of being accepted quickly and easily.

Offers That Don't Work

Even the best proposal won't be accepted if it isn't presented in a way that people can accept. Some ways to sabotage a good offer are:

1. Present it with contempt for the other party: "You may not see the value of this, but here's what I think . . ."
2. Give in to your fear that it won't be accepted: "You probably won't like this, but . . ."

3. Act in anger or with animosity: "I'm sick of dealing with this. Here's all I'm willing to do . . ."
4. Bully them or play King of the Mountain: "Take it or leave it. You're lucky to get this much . . ."

Honor yourself, your proposal, and your negotiating partners by making the offer in a way they can accept.

TECHNIQUE #82:
Prepare Your Team

Before you sit down at the table, make sure that your team members are aligned in their purpose and concentrating on the same goal. Your team includes the people on whose behalf you are negotiating (your company, your union, the management, your partners) and the people on your side who are coming with you to the negotiating session.

Before you go to the first session, be sure you have everything you need from the people whom you represent. Will you need their approval of your presentation? How much latitude do you have to negotiate? What can you give, and where must you stand firm? Get these questions answered before you go, and approach these in-house meetings with the same care and preparation that you bring to negotiations with the other side.

If others on your team are coming to the negotiating session with you, agree on which of you will be the leader, point person, or quarterback who guides the discussion and speaks for the group. Someone needs to be in charge and to call the shots.

Make sure everyone is clear about—

- Your bottom line.
- Your strategies.
- Strategies that you anticipate the other side will use.
- Points that you are willing to concede and those you're not.

When your team is aligned, working and thinking as one, you multiply the positive energy behind your proposal.

TECHNIQUE #83:
Don't Talk Before You're Prepared to Settle

If you start talking with the other side before you're ready to reach an agreement, you may wind up with less than you want. Before you start negotiating, be sure that—

1. You have done Step One and know your bottom line. You will do Step Two—Find out what they want and make them feel heard—in the course of the discussion. Don't go on to Step Three or start the actual give and take of negotiating until you are satisfied that Steps One and Two have been completed.
2. You are emotionally ready to settle. Don't proceed if you are angry or confused, or even if it just doesn't feel right yet.
3. You are logistically ready to settle. You may have to take external timetables into account. Can you settle before other projects have been finished, or before certain events have taken place?

Dave made the mistake of talking to the other side before he was prepared to settle, and regretted it. He had sustained a whiplash injury in a car accident, and his doctor had advised him not to settle the claim for at least six months because it might take that long for symptoms to show up. Dave agreed, but after about two months he got impatient. He decided he'd just sit down with the insurance company's representatives to see what they were thinking and get an idea of what kind of settlement he could expect.

Dave had satisfied none of the three conditions. He hadn't established his bottom line (since it was only two months after the injury, it was impossible to tell how much treatment he would need or what it would cost), and he wasn't ready either emotionally or logistically to settle. He was still angry, and it would take him at least six months to get the information he needed to make a good proposal.

Dave had never engaged in this type of negotiation before, but the people from the insurance company did it every day of the week. They were adept at getting people to settle early and low—and that's exactly what happened to Dave. He'd had no intention of settling that afternoon, but they shamed and cajoled him into it. They insinuated that he was trying to run a scam and that if he didn't settle then, he wouldn't get anything. They persuaded him that they would never offer more than they were offering that afternoon, and that it was in his best interest to take the money and run.

When you sit down to negotiate before you are ready to settle, you hand over all the control to the other people.

TECHNIQUE #84:
Demonstrate Visible Goodwill

It's natural for people to be wary when they begin a negotiation, especially if they don't know one another well. We've been taught to think of negotiations as adversarial win/lose situations, and to view others as opponents who threaten our ability to get what we want. Even under the best circumstances, people are inclined to be guarded at first.

You can minimize this defensiveness by demonstrating visible goodwill from the outset.

Let them know—by your attitude, your body language, and even your words if it's appropriate—that you want a fair agreement that benefits everyone. Demonstrate with a smile, a handshake, a compliment on some aspect of their endeavor, or a positive comment about the negotiation itself that you intend to make it as supportive and mutually beneficial as possible. Use words like "I've looked forward to doing business with you, and I'm sure we can reach an agreement that's good for both of us" or "My point of view is that when we both win, we both win double."

You can actually see people relax when they realize you aren't out to get them and don't want a bloodbath. Their body language loosens up, and you can watch the relief spreading across their faces.

Being generous with your goodwill—unilaterally, without being asked—costs you nothing. It doesn't weaken your position; it strengthens the bond between you, sets the stage for making an offer that they can accept, and lays the foundation for a good working relationship.

TECHNIQUE #85:
Remember That It's More Important to Be Perceived as Fair Than It Is to Be Well Liked

These two qualities—fairness and likability—are not mutually exclusive, but they are not always the same.

People would rather negotiate with someone they consider fair than with someone they like but don't necessarily trust. They give the fair person more respect, and are usually more flexible with him or her. People who are seen as more likable than fair may get invited out for drinks afterward, but they may not get the best agreement.

Liz was going to do a research project for Gene and Cliff's company, and they were in the process of working out a contract. Gene was a barrel of laughs—jovial, witty, and complimentary. Each time a problem emerged, he glossed it over with a joke, a personal comment, or flattery. Cliff didn't say much. He just kept jabbing at a calculator with the eraser of his pencil and occasionally pushing his glasses back up his nose, but he seemed to be making an honest effort to be fair so that they could all have what they wanted.

Liz trusted and respected Cliff more and more as the afternoon wore on, and grew increasingly suspicious of Gene. Cliff always came up with the bottom line, and seemed willing for her to make a fair profit. She felt comfortable conceding points to him that she wouldn't have felt comfortable conceding only to Gene, whose charm was wearing thin.

She was there to do business, and thought to herself that if Gene would go away and leave her and Cliff to hammer out the agreement, they could probably finish quickly and come up with a good contract.

It's important to be liked, but it's even more important to be perceived as fair.

TECHNIQUE #86:
Don't Bluff or Make Offers You Can't Live With If They Are Accepted

Bluffing can do two very harmful things:

1. It can stick you with an agreement that isn't acceptable. If you say, "I'd give a year's salary to get those terms," they may take you up on it.
2. It can undermine your credibility. Once people know you're a bluffer, they won't believe anything you say. It becomes almost impossible to negotiate in good faith.

Allison was looking for backers for her sandwich shop, and offered Dean 35 percent of the business if he would invest $100,000 or more. Her strategy was to start high and work down to something like $35,000 and 10 percent of the business. She never expected that he would give her the $100,000—or even that he had that much to give—and she never dreamed that she'd be stuck giving someone 35 percent of her business. He surprised her and she got caught in a deal that didn't work for her.

Never make an offer you hope they'll reject.

TECHNIQUE #87:
If You Don't Think You're Getting a Big Enough Piece of the Pie, Look for a Larger Pie

There is no shortage of pie in this world. You can always find something to sweeten the deal for yourself without asking the other person to give up much.

Hal knew that Candace had a limited budget for the salaries in her department, but she hadn't offered him enough. He knew that she'd cut him as big a piece as she could from the salary pie, so he started looking for a larger one and found it in benefits. The company did offer Candace a variety of perks for her employees: cars, upgraded insurance benefits at nominal cost, bonuses, a profit-sharing plan, extra paid vacation time, use of the company vacation home in San Diego.

Hal found a bigger pie by drawing up a list of the special benefits he needed to supplement his salary, and also asked for a six-month salary review. Candace was glad to give him what he wanted and impressed with his ability to find creative solutions.

Brock believed he needed at least $10,000 to travel to Chicago and present his time-management program to Hugh's employees, but Hugh was only prepared to offer $8,000. Brock wanted the job, so he found a bigger piece of pie for Hugh. He would present the program on Tuesday morning and then spend the afternoon working privately with individual employees on their specific needs. For that, Hugh was willing to pay $10,000.

Another way to find a larger pie is to keep the same provisions in an offer, but arrange them differently. They may not be willing to budge on the total cost, for instance, but they may be flexible about the timing or the amount of the payments.

TECHNIQUE #88:
Don't Panic If You Have Time Constraints;
Use the Pressure to Increase Your Effectiveness

It's called grace under pressure. Remember the power you have at your disposal with the three Triangle Talk steps and the techniques in this book. Adopt the attitude that you *will* complete the negotiation successfully, and that you'll do it in the time that's available to you.

Panic only wastes time, and produces no results. Stay calm, and remember that you can accomplish more, in less time, than you thought. You never know how much you can produce until you are challenged to go beyond your former limits.

Donna was the hospital administrator in charge of negotiating a new contract with the nurses' union. At ten o'clock in the morning, she got word that the union had voted to strike at midnight unless the hospital came up with an offer good enough to vote on by four o'clock that afternoon.

She could have panicked; instead, she called the woman who was representing the nurses and invited her over for a private chat. As they sat down to coffee, Donna said, "Look, I have the feeling this isn't really going to affect the outcome much; we're just going to get to wherever we were going *faster*. Let's cut to the chase. Tell me your absolute bottom line and I'll give you something they can vote on today."

Sometimes finding yourself on an unexpected deadline can grease the wheels of a negotiation and actually work to your advantage.

TECHNIQUE #89:
Don't Wait Until the End to Reach Agreement
on All Your Points

Keep the momentum going by deciding key issues and putting them in writing as you go along.

Moving items from the "Undecided" to the "Decided" column feels good and gives the negotiation a positive tone. It's clear that you're accomplishing something, and you can point to this success if people's energy starts to flag.

Each time you put a point in writing, you make it easier to decide the next issue. If you let all the decisions go until the end, the whole structure can cave in.

Barry and Elise could promote only three of their ten employees, and set aside an afternoon to make the decisions. Instead of talking for hours about all ten and then forcing themselves to make all the decisions in the last half hour, they talked about each employee individually and made a tentative decision: yes, no, or maybe.

One woman was clearly the best and definitely belonged in the yes category. Five other employees were definite nos. Of the four remaining, they made one a yes and three maybes.

Now their decision was much easier. They had two yesses, five definite nos, and three maybes. All they had to do was take the best employee among the three maybes and put him or her in the one remaining yes slot.

This technique is especially helpful when the discussion is somewhat adversarial. Even if no one signs the paper, writing down your decisions gives them more weight and certainty. People are less likely to waffle later.

TECHNIQUE #90:
Use Third-Party Mediators When Necessary

Sometimes emotions can become so volatile, and people so deeply entrenched in widely divergent positions, that it's impossible for the parties involved to sit down and work things out on their own.

When this happens, consider using a third-party mediator—either a neutral third party whom both of you trust, or a professional. Professional mediators are trained to work for both parties toward a solution, not for one party against the other, so the situation automatically becomes less adversarial.

Mediation has become an increasingly popular way to solve problems in business, law, divorce, labor, the arts, and many other fields—especially when the alternative is to hire expensive lawyers and let them fight it out in court.

TECHNIQUE #91:
Stay Flexible

This technique is the key to keeping a good negotiation moving, and to rescuing one that has gotten off the track. If you remember nothing else, remember these two things:

1. Stay alert to how others are reacting to you and your proposal.
2. Stay flexible so that you can self-correct and shift gears to do whatever will be most effective in that moment.

Use Steps One and Two to stay calm and grounded. When you know what you want and what they want, you have a rock-solid foundation and can afford to be flexible.

Keep watching and listening to their reactions. If you need to back off, do so. If you need to assert yourself and put your plan forward more forcefully, do that. Roll with the punches, and learn to change your attitude or approach quickly if necessary.

Negotiating for acceptance and a positive response is required in many situations—for example, when you are selling or presenting your ideas. Frances presented a popular sales seminar for a national consulting firm, and almost always got an enthusiastic response. One week in Denver, however, she could tell that it wasn't working. The thirty people in her audience sat stiffly, their faces tense and unresponsive, their arms and legs crossed. No one seemed to be present mentally.

After about an hour, Frances covered up her flip chart, closed the data book, and sat down on the table in front of the room. The participants continued to stare blankly at their notebooks.

"I don't know what's going on here," she said, "but I feel like I'm talking to an enormous fish tank. Can you help me out? Is this stuff completely uninteresting? Am I doing something wrong? What's going on?"

It turned out that the company was facing tremendous cutbacks and they'd just been told that 30 percent of the sales force would be let go. The people in her seminar were in shock. Everyone in the room was convinced that he or she would be let go, or that friends would be fired, or that the ship was sinking. The last thing they wanted to focus on was salesmanship.

First Frances let them talk about what was really bothering them. They needed to air their anger and fears before they could think about anything else. Then she had them write down what they wanted their personal futures to be with the company. Next she had them list how they could use this seminar to further those ends.

For the rest of the day, she used what was happening at the company in all her examples and illustrations. She kept their attention by constantly referring to their situation, and they came away with vivid memories of the seminar and a clear understanding of the principles it put forth.

Being flexible allowed Frances to turn a potential disaster into a victory for her students, herself, her company, and their company.

Making your offer can be the most challenging part of a negotiation, but you're on firm ground when you've done your homework with Steps One and Two and use these techniques.

EXERCISES

1. Which of these techniques did you use the last time you made a proposal? What was the result?
2. Which did you not use? How might they have helped?

REACH A SOLID CLOSURE

18

Nature brings us back to absolute truth whenever
we wander. If we learn the lesson, we lose both
the illusion and the pain it causes. If we resist,
misery remains.

—LOUIS AGASSIZ

After you've completed the three Triangle Talk steps and
reached your agreement, make sure that everybody is clear
about what happened and what is expected of him or her.

This makes your agreement real, solid, and concrete. It
brings a great sense of satisfaction and gives you something
to which you can refer if the terms of the agreement are ever
questioned.

Closure is whatever you do to nail down, finalize, or seal
the terms of your agreement. It may be drawing up a contract
and signing it, shaking hands, or writing a check for the down
payment—any physical act that signals the end of the negotiation and the beginning of the agreement.

This is the time when any uncertainty or loose ends become
obvious. Don't be afraid to ask about them. Get everything
clear now, while you are together and riding the "win." If you
feel uncertain or unsettled about closing, there may be something uncertain or unsettling in the agreement. Trust your
instincts, get an agreement that works, and reach a solid, final
closure.

TECHNIQUE #92:
Do Not Nibble or Be Nibbled

Once you have reached the agreement, don't go back and see whether you can get them to change just that one tiny little thing that you don't like. Stand behind the conditions to which you have agreed, and let them know that they can trust you to abide by those terms.

By the same token, don't let others "nibble" you. You can be firm at this point. The agreement probably won't fall through if you don't concede that small issue that they want you to go back and change "just this once."

Hope managed Cal's office, and he thought the office parties had gotten out of hand. There seemed to be no end to the occasions they celebrated: birthdays, anniversaries, babies, marriages, children's graduations, second cousins' engagements.

Cal met with Hope and explained the problem, and they agreed to limit the parties to Thanksgiving, Christmas, and the birthdays of people who actually worked in the office. As she was leaving, Hope turned around, flashed Cal a brilliant smile, and said, "Oh, I forgot. Esther starts maternity leave Monday and I know she's expecting a party Friday afternoon. We'll just do that one and then abide by the agreement."

Cal didn't want to be an ogre, but he knew that if he let Hope start nibbling their agreement, it wouldn't carry much weight. "I hate to be a heel," he said, "but I think we'd better stick to what we agreed. I'll be glad to explain the situation to Esther, and we can get her a gift and card instead."

Once you start nibbling, or allowing yourself to be nibbled, there is no end to the process. You can never be sure that you have an agreement, because you thought you had one before—and then it changed. The nibbling precedent erodes confidence and makes your agreement look like a piece of Swiss cheese.

Stand firm, and create an environment in which others must stand firm as well.

TECHNIQUE #93:
Offer to Prepare the Written Draft of the Agreement

Sometimes agreements need to be written down, even and especially when they are between friends or colleagues. In these cases, someone has to be responsible for drawing up the papers and putting your agreement into written form. There are two important advantages to doing this yourself:

1. You give something without being asked. You contribute time, energy, and secretarial support that the other parties don't.
2. You have some control over how the document reads, or at least how it is presented and prepared. You may actually be drafting the wording, or you may just be in charge of the typing. In any case, you can make sure that it is done to your standards. This may or may not make any real difference, but it can't hurt.

TECHNIQUE #94:
Honor Others Directly for Their Role in Coming to Terms

Acknowledge the respect you feel for them and the important part they played in the negotiation. Make sure that they experience the satisfaction of coming to an agreement. Speak to the relationship you have built, mention the specific contributions they made, and let them know that you appreciate their efforts.

If you clearly got the better bargain, don't rub it in or make them feel like victims. This kind of behavior will come back to haunt you; they will be looking for a way to return the favor someday.

TECHNIQUE #95:
Debrief with Colleagues

Affirm what went well and explore what you could have done better.

Establish a positive, supportive environment in which you can give one another this kind of feedback. Make sure that everyone feels comfortable talking about what could be improved, and that the recipients of these comments don't get offended or take the input personally. The point is to acknowledge a good job and prepare yourself to do an even better job next time.

Think of the old Sufi parable of the truth-seeker who climbed the mountain to the Wise One's cave and asked, "What is the secret of life?"

"Good judgment," the Wise One responded.

The truth-seeker rubbed his chin. "I see. How does one get good judgment?"

"Experience," said the Wise One.

"Ah yes, but how does one get experience?"

"Bad judgment," said the Wise One.

TECHNIQUE #96:
Do What You Said You Would Do,
and Then Do More

Matching your words and your actions builds trust and confidence. Let them see you doing what you said you would do as soon as possible, and then let them see you doing more.

Kent's catering company was chosen to provide box lunches for Beth's company's annual picnic, and he told her that he would have the contract in her hands by noon on Tuesday. It arrived at eleven-thirty, along with five complimentary box lunches for her and her staff.

In this unpredictable world, people feel comfor*table* with the reliable and comfor*ted* by the extra-reliable. Be someone they know they can trust absolutely, someone on whom they can rely to do your best and then some.

EXERCISES

1. Recall a time when you thought an agreement had been reached, and then it fell apart. What happened? Can you pinpoint which technique was left out?
2. What could you have done to make sure that agreement was solid?

MAKE GOOD AGREEMENTS A WAY OF LIFE

> Let us begin anew, remembering on both sides
> that civility is not a sign of weakness, that sincerity
> is always subject to proof. Let us never negotiate
> out of fear, but let us never fear to negotiate.
> —JOHN F. KENNEDY

Triangle Talk is not something to keep on a shelf and pull down only when you're negotiating a labor contract for a major automobile manufacturer. It is something to use every day, in personal areas and at work. It is meant to be a way of life, one that keeps your mind clear and your relationships honest, open, and mutually supportive.

TECHNIQUE #97:
Play the Inner Game of Agreement, and Affirm Your Life's Purpose Every Day

In the 1970s *The Inner Game of Tennis* by Michael Murphy brought psychological and spiritual principles to bear on the way a player feels and performs on a tennis court. The book made tennis seem like the game of life, and life seem like the game of tennis.

You can use Triangle Talk in the same way. Working with the three steps means that you are constantly making clear your current goals, setting new ones, examining your motivations, opening up to other people's perspectives, establishing new connections and relationships, solving problems, formulating good proposals, and putting yourself and your ideas forward in the most effective way.

Doing all this helps you—

- Stay centered.
- Become a more open and powerful person.
- Let go of limiting beliefs and habits.
- Expand into new levels of effectiveness.

Let Triangle Talk be a tool for making your whole life more exciting and fulfilling. Affirm your best and highest self as you let go of old scripts and reach toward new heights.

Some affirmations I use are:

- "I know the solution to this problem."
- "I know the answer to my deepest questions."
- "I care about others and expect the best from them."
- "I am quietly confident that whatever I set out to do can be achieved."

Also affirm your life's purpose every day, and let it guide all your smaller decisions. Your purpose reminds you why you are here and why you do what you do. It gives your words and actions greater meaning—for yourself and for others.

Keeping your purpose constantly before your eyes prevents you from getting stuck at comfortable plateaus. You are more willing to take risks when you know that they will further these aims.

TECHNIQUE #98:
Use the Buddy System

Agree with a friend or colleague to support one another in growing through the Triangle Talk approach.

You and your buddy can meet on a regular basis to—

- Strategize for situations you're facing.
- Discuss problems and offer feedback.
- Attend lectures and programs that will sharpen your skills.
- Share recommendations and reactions to books on related subjects.
- Use one another as consultants when you are in the midst of a difficult negotiation.
- Debrief with one another when it is over.

It makes an enormous difference when you have someone who actively supports your growth through Triangle Talk, someone who speaks the same language and can pat you on the back when you need it. Sharing also makes what you are accomplishing more real and concrete. You can move forward more quickly and easily with this kind of encouragement and companionship.

TECHNIQUE #99:
Give It Away

You really have something only when you can give it away. As you tell others about Triangle Talk, you get clearer and more certain yourself, and sharpen your own skills.

The added benefit is that you have more people in your life who use these same principles and know how to reach agreements more quickly and effectively.

Teaching someone golf or any other sport improves your own game. Telling someone about your vacation gives you a deeper experience of it. Sharing the Triangle Talk approach makes you a better negotiator and creates more people who can play at your level.

TECHNIQUE #100:
Practice, Practice, Practice

There is no substitute for practice—with Triangle Talk or anything else. What you practice projecting, you *are* projecting—and you become.

Every day, practice applying the three steps to some situation. Begin with people toward whom you feel neutral and work up to those for whom you have strong feelings. Watch your results. Look for what worked and what you can do better. You will be amazed at how quickly and dramatically you improve your ability to resolve problems, reach agreements, present yourself and your ideas effectively, and influence others' decisions.

Triangle Talk has given me a clarity in my agreements and a richness in my relationships that I hardly dreamed possible. My hope is that it will do the same for you.

THE FAST TRACK:
A Quick Guide to
the 100 Techniques
That Make Triangle Talk
Work Faster

For quick and easy reference, here are the 100 techniques that make the three Triangle Talk steps work better and faster:

1. Make "What do I want?" an automatic response.
2. Decide what you want by considering alternatives, then choosing one.
3. Create a specific, vivid mental image of what you want and describe it in one sentence.
4. Understand what is most important to you.
5. Develop a "larger than life" vision of yourself, your work, and your life.
6. Know how you see yourself, and how others see you.
7. Understand your power base.
8. Recognize your "hot buttons" and the hidden assumptions through which you see the world.
9. Find out what *they* want or mean, not what you would want or mean if you used the same words.
10. Don't deduce other people's intentions from your fears.

11. Don't assume you know what people want—or that they know what you want—just because you know one another well.

12. When you are with someone you like, check your assumptions more often, because you will tend to do it less.

13. See their world their way.

14. Learn to identify other people's assumptions, motivations, and prejudices, and what they consider threats or opportunities.

15. Remember that most people are not aware of their own prejudices, assumptions, and hot buttons.

16. Start out right: Make a good first impression.

17. Use nonverbal communication to establish rapport.

18. Play with your full deck.

19. Expect the best of yourself and others.

20. Cast a wide net with your initial questions.

21. "Columbo" them.

22. Avoid the "King of the Mountain" approach.

23. Ask open-ended questions.

24. Ask advice.

25. Send up trial balloons.

26. Listen actively.

27. Start out with oblique questions, then get increasingly specific and direct.

28. Appeal to their positive intent.

29. Use silence and pauses.

30. Go slow to go fast.

31. Ask direct questions.

32. Accept the situation *as it is*; don't pretend it's something different or try to make it what you *wish* it were.

33. Don't let emotional reactions or judgments about what they want sabotage the negotiation.

34. Avoid the temptation to talk sooner, higher, faster, and longer when you feel uncomfortable, angry, or threatened.

35. Use the AAAA Approach to create a bridge between you, not a gulf.

36. Acknowledge their concerns.

37. Use their language.
38. Avoid emotional terms that imply positive or negative reactions to what they say.
39. The more intense the conflict, the more strongly and explicitly you must acknowledge their position.
40. Speak to their needs first.
41. "Bridge" from their interests to your common interests to your interests.
42. Paint them a colorful, detailed picture.
43. Align with their personal or organizational values.
44. Position your proposal by using "social proof," authoritative endorsements, likability, and appeals to their self-image.
45. Give something away up front, without being asked.
46. Sandwich your controversial or bad news between two pieces of good news.
47. Choose your point of emphasis.
48. Lavish "Velcro praise" on others.
49. Make sharp contrasts.
50. Move from the larger to the smaller picture.
51. Remember the Two-Choice Rule.
52. Use the Rule of Scarcity.
53. Let conflict surface when it exists, but keep it under control and don't dig in your heels.
54. Remember that the problem is not *the other person*; it's how you react to one another in the situation.
55. Remember that you always have only three choices: (1) accept the situation; (2) leave; or (3) change your behavior.
56. Don't let others determine your behavior or your self-worth.
57. Discover an admirable motive, especially when you don't think they have one.
58. Give the kind of energy you want to get back, and pay attention to the qualities in others that you want to see more.
59. Remember that men and women are different.
60. Develop a semipermeable membrane.
61. Contrast the disadvantages of quitting with the benefits of continuing.

62. Keep the momentum going by reviewing the progress you've made so far.
63. P-A-C-E yourself.
64. At each step, give people a stake in the outcome.
65. Point out that no situation has to be win-lose.
66. Be courteous and preserve mutual respect, especially when you least feel like it.
67. Identify the people who bother you most and learn to manage your encounters with them.
68. Find out why they upset you and disarm that mechanism.
69. Tell the people you see regularly what you will and will not tolerate.
70. Act, don't react, when meeting new people who trigger negative feelings.
71. Let go of the vibrating pole.
72. Use the Ten-Minute Rule.
73. Stop the chain reaction.
74. Use the Jimmy Swaggart approach.
75. "Fog" to avoid or postpone a response.
76. Use the Messy Desk Solution.
77. Shift the spotlight.
78. Empower others, don't coerce or manipulate them.
79. Pinpoint your specific power sources.
80. Avoid power plays.
81. Take the power you need.
82. Prepare your team.
83. Don't talk before you're prepared to settle.
84. Demonstrate visible goodwill.
85. Remember that it's more important to be perceived as fair than it is to be well liked.
86. Don't bluff or make offers you can't live with if they are accepted.
87. If you don't think you're getting a big enough piece of the pie, look for a larger pie.
88. Don't panic if you have time constraints; use the pressure to increase your effectiveness.
89. Don't wait until the end to reach agreement on all your points.
90. Use third-party mediators when necessary.

91. Stay flexible.
92. Do not nibble or be nibbled.
93. Offer to prepare the written draft of the agreement.
94. Honor others directly for their role in coming to terms.
95. Debrief with colleagues.
96. Do what you said you would do, and then do more.
97. Play the inner game of agreement, and affirm your life's purpose every day.
98. Use the buddy system.
99. Give it away.
100. Practice, practice, practice.

Kare Anderson is a frequent speaker and consultant to groups as diverse as CBS, Ringling Bros., the American Association of Medical College Deans, Nomura Securities, and AT&T.

She speaks on:

1. "Everyday Persuasion and Negotiation Skills: Selling Your Ideas and Winning Agreement" (based on the topic of this book)

2. "Make Yourself Memorable: Communicating with Skill and Power

3. "Synthesizer Leader Skills: Trends in MVP Team Play"

4. "Using All Five Senses to Attract and Keep Customers"

5. "Geting Your Message Out: Building Clout, Visibility and Public Support"

6. "'YES' Triggers of Influence: What Makes People Instinctively Agree?"

7. "Minimizing Brief, Frequent Encounters Between Buyers and Sellers"

For more information on her programs and related audio and video tapes contact her at (800) 488-KARE (5273); (415) 389-9746; fax: (415) 389-0434.

INDEX